J J Williams

the life and times of a rugby legend

*Dedicated to my wife Jane
and my children
Kathryn, James and Rhys*

J J Williams

the life and times of a rugby legend

J J Williams with Peter Jackson

First impression: 2015

© Copyright JJ Williams and Y Lolfa Cyf., 2015

The contents of this book are subject to copyright, and may
not be reproduced by any means, mechanical or electronic,
without the prior, written consent of the publishers.

The publishers wish to acknowledge the support of
Cyngor Llyfrau Cymru

Front cover photograph: Getty Images
Back cover photograph: Emyr Young
Cover design: Y Lolfa

ISBN: 978 1 78461 142 2

Published and printed in Wales
on paper from well-maintained forests by
Y Lolfa Cyf., Talybont, Ceredigion SY24 5HE
website www.ylolfa.com
e-mail ylolfa@ylolfa.com
tel 01970 832 304
fax 832 782

Contents

CHAPTER 1

Nantyffyllon

Peter Jackson

THE LAST SHOTS of the Second World War had still to be fired when an astrological phenomenon began to illuminate the skies above the scarred landscape of the south Wales coalfield.

Out of the darkness of a global conflict so terrible that it claimed up to 80 million lives, new stars appeared in the firmament high above the full spectrum of the rugby belt straddling the breadth of the country from east to west. Each one marked the birth of those whose collective lives would change the pecking order of world rugby as it had never been changed before, or since.

What made each and every one different wasn't merely that they won Grand Slams for Wales. As Lions in the early 1970s, they won successive Test series against the All Blacks and the Springboks, world-beaters in the widest sense of the phrase.

There were eight of them in total and the first, Barry John, arrived at the end of the first week of 1945 in the Carmarthenshire village of Cefneithin. The boy who grew up to be crowned 'The King' at a makeshift coronation before the end of the 1971 Lions tour of New Zealand would also be rugby's first superstar.

One month later, in another village in the same county, Gerald Davies entered the world, a bit further west from

Cefneithin at Llansaint. Within the next four years the galaxy shining down from the heavens would be complete.

Bobby Windsor and Mervyn Davies were born in the first and last months of 1946 in Newport and Swansea respectively; Gareth Edwards at Gwaencaegurwen in 1947 and Phil Bennett at Felinfoel the following year, in between the advent of not one John Williams but two.

By the time John Peter Rhys Williams was born in Bridgend 24 hours after St David's Day 1949, John James Williams had beaten him to it. The convergence of their careers some 20-odd years later led to a severe abbreviation of their names which would make each instantly recognisable the rugby world over.

One became JPR, the other JJ. The initials elevated them to a status all of their own, ensuring the letters became as famous in rugby circles as FDR and JFK have long been to students of the American presidency.

JJ's entry into the world, on April Fool's Day in 1948, ensured that his village did not miss out on the star treatment. Down the road at the Old Parish, home of the nearest first-class rugby club, Maesteg rose to the occasion in magnificent fashion completing the 1949–50 season without defeat. Under the captaincy their Lions scrum half Trevor Lloyd, 'The Invincibles' played 43 matches, winning 37, drawing the other six, scoring 426 points and conceding a miserly 110.

Nantyffyllon is a hard name to pronounce and a harder one to spell but not for those who know their sporting history. It was home to the most successful captain in the history of Welsh international football. David Lloyd Bowen took Wales into the quarter-finals of the World Cup in Sweden during the summer of 1958 when only a scruffy debut goal by a 17 year old called Edson Arantes do Nascimento, later shortened to Pelé, prevented them from advancing to the last four.

For Bowen, who as a boy had suffered from rheumatic

fever, any kind of sporting success represented triumph over adversity. The story goes that he won a pair of football boots in a raffle, decided to get some wear out of them and never looked back.

A surveyor in the mining industry, he became a professional footballer later than usual, joining Northampton Town in his early 20s rather than his teens before transferring to Arsenal. After captaining the Gunners, Bowen rejoined Northampton as player-coach and then embarked on a feat which had not been done before.

'The Cobblers,' unheralded and unsung, had languished in the lower divisions of the Football League as if resigned to their lot. Bowen changed all that, taking them from the Fourth Division to the First in consecutive seasons. And then, as if to show that it really was a load of old cobblers and that Newton's theory about what goes up must come down applies just as effectively to soccer management, he took them all the way back again.

He wasn't the first from Nantyffyllon to make it against the odds. William Davies left as a boy when his family emigrated to America and settled in a little place in Pennsylvania called Roscoe, 25 miles south of Pittsburgh.

They called him 'Wee Willie', a flyweight boxer who fought anywhere and everywhere at a time when prize-fighting in the United States was never busier, nor more popular.

Fight fans all over the States knew back then of another Welsh flyweight – Jimmy Wilde, variously lauded as 'The Mighty Atom', 'The Tylorstown Terror' and 'The Ghost with the Hammer in his Hand'. Wilde, seven stone wringing wet, had his last fight at the Polo Grounds in New York on 18 June 1923 against Pancho Villa, a valiant but unsuccessful attempt to prevent his Filipino opponent claiming the world title.

One year later, Davies would be denied a place in American

trials for the 1924 Olympiad because he had not been born in the USA. In nine years from the mid-1920s to the early 1930s, Davies had 176 professional contests, winning 129 and drawing 17. His record included an eliminator for the then vacant world flyweight title which he lost on points.

Between them, Bowen and Davies took Nantyffyllon to football stadia throughout the UK, to boxing venues in America from Madison Square Garden in New York to all over Pennsylvania, Ohio and southern Canada.

JJ took it farther afield, across new frontiers to places where they had never heard of Nantyffyllon, to the revered rugby cathedrals of New Zealand and South Africa. Most unusually of all, he would take it to places like the prison on Robben Island where Nelson Mandela and the other ANC political prisoners cheered the Lions as they listened to radio commentaries of their record-breaking series in South Africa in 1974.

JJ

NANTYFFYLLON IS A coal-mining village situated a mile north of Maesteg in the Llynfi valley where thousands used to work underground in six collieries. I was born there at No. 1 Garnwen Terrace on the first of April 1948 in the Chinese Year of the Rat and you could say that my entry into the world provided a double cause for celebration in the neighbourhood.

Three days earlier at Twickenham, on the Easter Monday, France had beaten England 15-nil in the last match of that year's Five Nations Championship, a result which left our old rivals lumbered with the wooden spoon. One auspicious occasion followed by another, not that I was aware of either at the time.

My father, Glyn, drove a bus for a living, from the top of the valley to Maesteg and back every day of his working life.

My mother, Lizzie, had given birth to three sons years before I came along as an afterthought – 17 years after my eldest brother Terry, 12 years after Ken and seven years after Peter.

Maybe that explains why I've always been in such a rush. I suppose I've been running all my life, on the rugby field, the athletics track, and then establishing my own business. It's almost as if I've been driven by a compulsion to make up for lost time.

Births in the early post-war years usually took place at home, not in hospital. My mother ran the home as a housewife for whom nothing was too much trouble. Sunday at Saron Welsh Independent Chapel in High Street, Maesteg, was always the highlight of her week.

Sundays in my youth were almost as if they had come straight out of a scene from *How Green Was My Valley*. Everyone wore their Sunday best and went to worship as a family. As a boy, I went to chapel three times every Sunday until I was 15 and then I cut it back to twice a day, morning and evening until I left home three years later to start a teacher-training course in Cardiff.

I have nothing but happy memories of growing up in Garnwen Terrace. Our house was open all the time with a steady flow of people coming in or going out, what with my brothers' friends from the rugby club and all the chapel people who called to see my parents.

There was a real sense of community in Nantyffyllon in the 1950s, a neighbourliness which gave you a feeling of safety and security. We locked the front door at night but it was never locked during the day because it was unheard of then for anyone from down the street to walk into a neighbouring house and steal something.

My home meant that when the time came for me to start primary school, I only had to walk 50 yards or so. Getting there meant passing the Welsh-speaking school. What a mistake that was, but back then going to a Welsh school in preference to an English-speaking one was considered taboo. How attitudes have changed.

I owe a debt of gratitude to many people for the help they have given me over the course of my life and Mr Eifion Williams, a teacher at Nantyffyllon Junior School, was one of the first. It was he who introduced me to rugby union and he who made sure that I never lacked encouragement.

Under his guidance, our team reached the final of the Schools' Valleys Cup, quite an achievement for a school as small as ours. I was the outside half, goal-kicker, tactical general and in charge of just about everything else, except the half-time oranges. I'd have done that gladly if only we could have afforded one or two.

Ever since I can remember, I've been interested in running and I soon realised I was faster than most of the other boys. That was no surprise because my brothers were as fanatical about athletics in the summer as they were about rugby in the winter.

Friends of the family always reckoned that Ken was the most talented of the Williams quartet which was really saying something. There's always been a fair bit of politics swirling round in under-age Welsh rugby and it was probably worse when my brothers were growing up. Ken would certainly vouch for that because, for some mysterious reason, he never got his Wales Youth cap.

We couldn't understand it then and here we are more than half a century later still none the wiser. As befitting his status as one of the best young centres in the country, Ken captained the Probables against the Possibles. They won the trial by a country mile and yet when the Wales team was announced, Ken was the only one of the Probables not to be picked. Work that one out.

Fate then took a hand in the form of a knee injury which

was serious enough to finish Ken as far as rugby was concerned. He took up golf, even though few lads of his age did that because it was considered an upper- or middle-class game.

Ken took to it as if to the manor born. In next to no time he'd gone from complete novice to a handicap of three. I thought at one stage that he could have made it as a professional but he decided against that and, as a past captain, became one of the pillars of Maesteg Golf Club.

On the last Friday of June 2015, he and his wife, Rita, survived the massacre in the Tunisian resort of Sousse which claimed the lives of more than 30 holidaymakers, the vast majority of them British. Rita had a particularly miraculous escape.

They'd been shopping early that morning and were strolling along the beach when they heard gunfire. People were shouting for them to run for their lives and, as they did so, Rita felt a bullet graze her head. She turned to Ken and said: 'I've been shot.' It was only later that she saw a bullet hole in her sunhat and realised how terrifyingly close she came to losing her life.

Terry, my eldest brother, wasn't a sportsman but he was a wonderful supporter of mine when I was growing up, a real rock. My father suffered badly from asthma and so my older brothers were the ones who made sure I got to all the rugby matches. Peter set the standard in those days, playing second row for Bridgend and gaining a Welsh international trial. He also found time to become Welsh schools' champion in the triple jump.

He had been a left-footed outside half as a schoolboy and a specialist sevens player. Then he went to Caerleon College and a few drinking sessions slowly but surely turned him into a larger specimen capable of holding his own among the hard men of the second row.

Peter's success wasn't limited to on the field. He went on to coach Maesteg, taking them to successive Whitbread Merit Table titles as Welsh champions in the late 1970s. He also coached the Welsh schools under-18s with outstanding results, including wins over Australia and New Zealand.

After passing my 11+ examination, I went to Maesteg Grammar School as it was then, Maesteg Comprehensive as it is now. For the three years from the age of 11 to 14 I hardly played any competitive rugby, making do instead with inter-house matches.

In hindsight it proved to be a blessing in disguise. It meant I wasn't exposed to any dreary squad sessions and so, instead of running the risk of losing some of my natural flair and feel for the game, I was allowed to develop at my own pace in my own time.

Again, as with Mr Williams at junior school in Nantyffyllon, I was fortunate to come under the guidance of another rugby master, Mr David Brown, who was a stickler for teaching the core skills.

All those painstaking lessons devoted to learning the skills of passing, kicking, tackling, sidestepping, swerving and so forth stood me in really good stead for the rest of my rugby days. If only today's school curriculum would allow boys the time to learn such skills, the standards in the modern game would be rather higher than they are today.

David Brown also saw to it that virtually the entire school rugby team took part in athletics and in that respect he was a man ahead of his time. The enthusiasm he created could be reflected in the fact that the school needed three buses to transport all the competitors, boys and girls, to the Glamorgan County Athletics Championships.

I hurled myself into it so that it became a big part of my sporting life. For the three years from 15 to 18, I played rugby all winter and did athletics all summer. I probably thought I would have a better chance of representing my country as a sprinter than as an outside half.

The Wales under-15 schoolboy team passed me by, probably on the basis that I was too small and spindly. By the time I reached sixth form I had filled out a bit. I was ready to make my bid for a Welsh Secondary Schools' cap, as an outside half.

In those days it was quite an achievement to get through the local district trials because there were so many of them and any one could you bring crashing down. I must have got through about eight trial matches by the time I got to the final trial. This was the big one – Wales against The Rest on the side of a Monmouthshire valley at a place called Blaina, famous as the birthplace of a Wales outside half who captained the Lions, David Watkins.

So I went up with Mr Brown and my brothers in our humble Ford Prefect car. We'd just pulled into the car park when along came a Rolls Royce. I'd never seen a car as big and as a grand because Nantyffyllon wasn't exactly crawling with them back in my youth, just as it isn't crawling with them today.

A few boys jumped out of the back of the Rolls followed by the boy who was to play behind me at full back. We had never seen him play before but we thought he must be more than a bit useful because he never had to bother with all the district trials. Instead he jumped straight out of Millfield School into the prospective Wales team.

And that was when I first met John Peter Rhys Williams, never dreaming for a second that our careers would take off simultaneously on the steepest of upward curves right to the very pinnacle of the sport. The man behind the wheel of the Rolls Royce that day, John's father Dr Peter Williams, had a massive influence in making his son the player he became.

He gave JPR what I always considered to be his greatest strength, an unshakeable belief in his ability to out-perform whomever he ran into on the other side. I remember Dr Peter striding into the dressing room before that day at Blaina and making a beeline for me.

He pointed to my under-nourished biceps. 'Tell your Dad to buy you some steak and build you up,' he said.

Steak? My immediate thought was to ask him: What's a steak? Whether it was shyness or a reluctance to show my ignorance, I said nothing.

As a boy, I cannot ever recall eating anything as expensive as a steak. The nearest I ever got was a steak and kidney pie which we had every once in a while as a treat. It made me think, but I put it out of my mind to concentrate on doing myself justice in the trial.

Although this was the first time I'd met JPR, I had heard of him through his exploits as a tennis player. His success on the court had generated a lot of publicity locally, as had my success on the sprint track. In terms of background, we were worlds apart. We talked briefly about the importance of the match without saying much. JPR exuded a quiet confidence then which never changed in all the years we played together.

The trial went well for both of us. We grabbed a bite to eat and went our separate ways in our different cars, aware that there was nothing more we could do other than wait for the team to be selected.

Before it was announced, I had been devastated by a family tragedy on the second day of December 1966. My Dad passed away after a valiant battle against the ravages of asthma and it made us all realise the precious but fragile nature of life.

He had been terribly ill for some time, sitting in the corner of the front room gasping for breath. Towards the end he could scarcely walk ten yards without having to stop but every so often he would find the strength and the courage to get back to work despite his dreadful disease.

If you didn't work in those days, you didn't get paid. That

was one of the harsher facts of everyday life and people who complain today ought to count their blessings and think twice. My father's illness put a terrible strain on both my parents.

He was only 60 when he died, no age at all. The timing was particularly cruel because it meant that my father would never see me play for Wales and I knew how proud he would have been had he only lived a little longer. His death cast a dark shadow over our lives.

My mother never got over it. She died of a broken heart two years and two days after she lost her husband, on 4 December 1968. She passed away sitting in her chair in the kitchen but not before she had gone out of her way to encourage me in my ambition to win a Welsh Secondary Schools' cap, reminding me of how proud my dad would have been.

She took his place. My mother would always be there whenever and wherever I competed as an athlete and more often than not she'd bring a load of friends and relatives to ensure I never wanted for any lack of support.

When I won my cap at No. 10 for the Secondary Schools against Wales Youth at Stradey Park, my opposite number was a short, dark, unusual-looking bloke from Felinfoel by the name of Philip Bennett. He also happened to have the most outrageous sidestep off his left foot that I had ever seen.

The match pitted the best of the Welsh schoolboys against the best of those boys who had left school early, like Phil. I could not have wished for a better debut at Stradey, a magical place which certainly had a magical effect on me in granting me a lifetime of bragging rights over my rival.

We won 9–6 and Phil still cannot believe that I dropped the goal that made all the difference. He always claims it was one of the biggest flukes he had seen but sometimes even the greats talk a load of old baloney. If that was a big fluke, as 'Benny' reckons, then how come I dropped another goal against France Schools a few weeks later?

That Welsh schools' team contained three more boys who would go on to play for Wales – Allan Martin and the late John Bevan from Aberavon, and the London Welsh centre, Keith Hughes. For the last schools' international of that season, England at Cardiff Arms Park, the selectors switched me to the wing. Believe it or not, I had never played there. I saw myself as an outside half and nothing else.

My opposition wing that day for England was none other than Keith Fielding who made a big name for himself in both codes, Union and League. The one consolation about being moved out to the wing was that I would get a brand-new jersey with a different number. Or so I thought...

Imagine, then, how gutted I felt when a letter arrived containing the number 14 and instructions to stitch it on to the old jersey in place of the number ten. Just as I had got the winning drop goal against the Welsh Youth and the French schools, so I was lucky enough to get the decisive try against England, and I scored in a way which I suppose became my trademark – chasing a kick which bounced up kindly allowing me to sprint 50 metres to touch down under the posts.

So two of my last matches before taking the plunge into the first-class club game were at grounds that would provide me with unforgettable memories of wonderful occasions. Mind you, had someone told me then that I would be back at Stradey in the Llanelli team that beat the All Blacks and, on top of that, back at the Arms Park winning two Grand Slams, I would have had him certified.

As a teenager I must have spent as much time, if not more, watching rugby as I did playing it. Every Saturday I could be found watching my local team, Nantyffyllon. If the first XV were playing away, I'd watch the seconds and vice versa. Sometimes I'd even jump on the team bus but not before I'd made sure that they would be coming straight back after the game. Had I been late, my mother would have gone berserk.

It wasn't until towards the end of my school years that I made my debut for the Nantyffyllon first team. I was absolutely thrilled to be representing my village club, so much so that if the seconds were a man short, I was only too happy to fill in.

I only played a dozen matches for the firsts but I was lucky enough to break the club try-scoring record, not as a wing but as an outside half. I got four in one match, against Llanharan who were then one of the strongest second-class clubs in Wales.

One of those tries came from our own in-goal area. I reckon I must have sidestepped, swerved and chipped the whole Llanharan XV, some of them more than once! But it wasn't all a bed of roses, as I found out during the return fixture at Llanharan a fortnight later. They were waiting for me and not just on the pitch.

Instead of four more tries, I landed four drop goals, just in case anyone thought I was a one-trick pony! During the game when one of my touch kicks cleared the fence around the pitch, I skipped over it like a hurdler to retrieve the ball.

A little old lady handed me the ball but she was in no mood to compliment me on my goal-kicking. 'We've had a gutsful of you lot,' she said, whereupon she whacked me over the head with her umbrella and I thought for a moment that I was going to be knocked out. Then, in case I hadn't got the message that this was no playful prank, she said: 'Don't ever come back here again.'

Talk about a reality check. The incident provided a perfect illustration that Welsh rugby at all levels has always been a tough nut to crack. Even the smaller clubs could be as tough as old boots. As for Llanharan, I never did go back, not because I was afraid of being assaulted by the same little old lady with the umbrella but because the opportunity never arose. I had nothing but respect for the club, especially their more mature female fans!

My next decision was over which club to join. Maesteg and Bridgend were the two closest to home and while Maesteg didn't show that much interest in me, Bridgend did. A friend of my brother Ken, Ralph Parker, came to the house one evening and said he had called to take me to training with Bridgend at the Brewery Field.

Ralph didn't come on his own. He brought Keith Bradshaw, the biggest star at Bridgend during the Sixties and an international centre who kicked goals from all over the place. He made a real impression on me, promising to look after me in training. How could I possibly go wrong?

I was the Great Britain schools' sprint champion and confident I could handle whatever Bridgend threw at me in training, which only goes to show how wrong you can be. I thought I was fit but I obviously wasn't anywhere near fit enough because halfway through the session, Keith came up to me with some harsh words of advice.

'Young man, if you want to make it in first-class rugby,' he began. 'If you are serious about wanting to get to the top, then you're going to have to get yourself fit.'

Keith's words took the wind out of my sails. Bridgend's coach, Illtyd Williams, was a man way ahead of his time because he imposed a regime which placed a heavy emphasis on physical fitness. Far from being put off, the challenge gave me a powerful source of motivation.

More than anything, I wanted to play in the same back division as Keith Bradshaw. Unfortunately Keith damaged his knee very badly just before the season began and that put the kibosh on my ambition of playing alongside one of my heroes who passed away in February 2014 at the age of 74.

In spite of the question marks over my fitness, I made the Bridgend squad for the new season and that was a really big deal. I was thrilled and honoured to be playing not for just any old first-class club but one that had an envied reputation for playing the game as it was meant to be played, using all 15 men all the time.

For all the attractions of rugby, I never let it distract me from my athletics and the pursuit of Welsh and British titles. Under David Brown's expert guidance, I won three Welsh races at the annual championships in Colwyn Bay and broke the record in all three – 100 yards, 200 yards and relay.

It meant I was running faster than some star names who had gone before me, like Ken Jones, Ceri Jones and Terry Davies – all outstanding sprinters who went on to become international rugby players. Ken Jones, of course, won an Olympic medal for Great Britain at Wembley in 1948, the year I was born.

I also got my first taste of international competition that same season, representing Great Britain against France at under-20 level in both sprints and the relay. The following year, 1967, came during the metrication of the UK, from yards, feet and inches to metres and centimetres. In the switch-over all pre-metric records disappeared. Why, I am not sure, but whenever I go to any track-and-field meetings anywhere in the UK, my name is nowhere to be seen in the record book.

My first British schools' event took me to Belfast and that was where I met a fellow by the name of Gareth Edwards. I had seen him but not met him in the Glamorgan County Championships where he won the long jump and hurdles before gaining a scholarship to Millfield School.

That stamped him as an exceptional athlete but I only

realised how exceptional when I read that he had won the English Schools' 220-yard hurdles title at Millfield. Because of what he achieved on the other side of the Severn Bridge, then newly-built, we were on opposite sides at that British schools' meeting.

For the first and only time in his life, Gareth Edwards represented England. He travelled to Northern Ireland with the Wales team and he travelled back with us but, for the serious business of competing, he was on the other side wearing a white vest with a red rose on it.

I've been to his home many times over the years and I always make a point of ribbing him about the time he ran for England. I always make a point, too, of trying to find his vest with the red rose in his display cabinet but to no avail. It's there somewhere and one day I shall find it...!

At the end of that summer in 1966, I was 18 and about to embark on the next stage of my life, a three-year teachers' training course at what was then Cardiff College of Education, now Cardiff Metropolitan University. But before my studies began I had a call from a senior lecturer at the College who was also renowned for his rugby coaching, Leighton Davies.

In the student world, he was 'Mr Rugby'. He asked me to join the other college boys for training at Bridgend in preparation for an annual sevens tournament at Kelso in the Scottish Borders, the spiritual home of the seven-a-side game. In my school days, I used to watch the College teams train and I would gaze in admiration at their green tracksuits.

They always looked the part and now, all of a sudden, I was one of them, heading for Kelso in a team which included Gareth Edwards. He was a year older than me (still is come to think of it!) and people tend to forget that he was already a superstar almost right from the start as the youngest captain of Wales at the age of 20.

At the Kelso tournament, I managed to chip in with two or

three tries a game and before we knew it we were in the final and up against a Gala team who were not about to let a bunch of College kids give them the runaround.

One month later, I got down to work as a student at college in the Cardiff suburb of Cyncoed. I joined the rugby and athletics clubs right away with my immediate ambition to make the College first XV. Athletics could wait until the following summer.

Many of my fellow students were boys whom I had competed alongside at schoolboy rugby matches and athletics' meetings. Suddenly, the level of competition had gone up several notches with the presence of three or four schoolboy international outside-halves at the College, all vying for the one spot.

The probability was that I would have to move, if not a little further out then a whole lot further out. It was a sign of the College's rising status that their fixture list included London Welsh, then *the* club in the British Isles with their own galaxy of Welsh Lions whose impact would stretch soon enough all the way to the far side of the world.

The day we played the Exiles at Old Deer Park in London was the day I appeared at centre and found myself playing against the ringmaster of all those stars, John Dawes. Whenever we have met in the years since that match way back in the 1960s, I've pulled his leg about how I gave him the runaround. I did nothing of the kind but I thought if I kept telling John often enough that I did, he might begin to think there was a grain of truth in it.

John, or 'Syd' as we called him, the nickname being an abbreviation of his first Christian name, was the central figure in making London Welsh what they were in those golden days – the most admired club team in the game. Little did I know then that he was to play a massive role in my development, coaching me for years with Wales and with the 1977 British and Irish Lions in New Zealand.

Tactics were evolving rapidly, especially in midfield with the introduction of the 'crash ball' move as mastered by Ray Gravell. For a greyhound like me, there was never going to be a future as a centre, so eventually I realised that if I was going to make it big as a rugby player, it would be on the wing or nowhere.

I went on mixing my studies with rugby and athletics. I'd train with the first XV twice a week, play on a Saturday and train with the athletics team on the other non-rugby nights, including Sundays. By then I had met an Olympic champion, Lynn Davies, in his capacity as a lecturer at the College.

His brilliant achievement in winning the gold medal in the long jump at the 1964 Olympiad in Tokyo made him more famous in world terms than any other Welsh sportsman. Inevitably, he began to have a big influence on me in terms of convincing me that I had a bigger future on the sprint track than on the rugby field.

I was always a rugby player first and foremost but the persuasive presence of an 18-carat superstar like Lynn meant that I was being pulled in opposite directions. Leighton Davies, the College's rugby coach, had been adamant from day one.

'You play rugby for the College,' he kept telling me. 'And, one day, you will play for Wales. Mark my words.'

Lynn's advice was equally definite and forthright: 'Concentrate on your sprinting and you'll have a chance of going to the next Commonwealth Games.'

On top of all that, Bridgend wanted me to play for them every Saturday, instead of the College. Decisions, decisions, decisions.

At the end of my first year at College, in the spring of 1967, I did play for Bridgend, in the final of the Snelling Sevens, Welsh rugby's leading seven-a-side tournament. This was no mickey mouse event. This was a major event in front of more than 30,000 spectators at Cardiff Arms Park.

And guess what? Bridgend won it for the first time in their history and I walked off with my first trophy in senior rugby, the Bill Everson award as the player of the tournament. Those decisions had still to be made and my father's tragic passing some years earlier meant I had lost the person I would have turned to first for advice.

Years later, in a complete role-reversal, I found myself trying to give my son, Rhys, some fatherly words of wisdom when he had to choose between athletics and rugby. It was easier for Rhys because he was then on the verge of establishing himself as a top-class international athlete.

Back at Cardiff Training College in the second half of the 1960s I met a beautiful girl from Carmarthen called Jane who just happened to be in the same year as me at the same College. She knew nothing about sport and I always remember going into Cardiff city centre on one of our first Saturday night dates and buying a copy of the *Sports Echo,* the Pink 'Un, which was better known in the winter as the *Football Echo.*

Anyway, on that particular Saturday there was a photograph of me on the front winning the Welsh sprint title at the national championships that afternoon. Jane glanced at the picture. 'Is that you?' she said. 'Well, I never...'

She thought I was just some rugby player who got the odd game for the College first team. Well, I never...

CHAPTER 2

Up and Running

Peter Jackson

ON THE RICHTER scale of momentous events in what could be loosely referred to as peace time, 1968 registers higher than most. It was, after all, the year of Dr Martin Luther King's assassination in Memphis, Tennessee, of student riots in Paris and Soviet tanks rolling into Prague to crush the Czech revolution.

In Vietnam, Viet Cong soldiers attacked the US Embassy in Saigon. In America, President Johnson decided against running for a second term, clearing the way for the entry to the White House of 'Tricky Dickie,' alias Richard Nixon.

In Mexico, the Olympic Games signalled the end of Lynn Davies' reign as long-jump champion, not because he flopped but because of a human freak by the name of Bob Beamon. He flew so far from take-off to landing that they ran out of tape measure before recording the distance at an unprecedented 29 feet, two inches. Lynn the Leap had been eclipsed by Beamon the flying demon.

Back home in Britain, they completed the final stretch of the nation's first motorway, the M1. On another road, at Hockenheim in Germany, the great racing driver from the Scottish borders, Jim Clark, lost his life in a crash.

Apartheid reared its ugly head at Lord's, the headquarters of cricket. South Africa's refusal to accept an England tour party that included the Cape Coloured, Basil D'Olivieira of

Worcestershire, led to the cancellation of that winter's MCC visit.

By then the Lions had completed their tour of South Africa, the four home rugby unions barely bothering to stop and think about the morality of giving succour to a despised regime. Had they done so, they might conceivably have saved themselves from failing to win any of the four-Test series against the Springboks.

On a lighter note, a new comedy show made its debut on BBC television, *Dad's Army*. It was probably nothing more than a happy coincidence, or an unhappy one, that France chose to mark the appearance of the bumbling Captain Mainwaring by winning the Grand Slam for the first time.

They won it, what's more, at Cardiff Arms Park, beating Wales 14–9 thanks in no small part to their fraternal half backs the Camberabero brothers, Guy and Lilian. Wales, spared the wooden spoon thanks to the pointless Scots, finished the Five Nations Championship in urgent need of a few creative sparks, as reflected in the failure of their threequarters to score more than the one solitary try, by Keri Jones of Cardiff in a 5–0 home win over Scotland.

Between 1968 and 1971, Wales capped no fewer than 13 wings. They found a pearl in Maurice Richards, the Cardiff wing from Ystrad in the Rhondda whose four tries against England at the Arms Park in April 1969 has left an indelible mark in the annals of Anglo-Welsh history.

Regrettably for Wales, his feat only accelerated the end of his Union career. Rugby league duly picked him off, Salford making Richards an offer which he found too good to turn down. Whatever the exact money, it proved to be seriously smart business by Salford because over 14 years from the late 1960s to the early 1980s, Maurice Richards scored 297 tries from 498 matches.

Without him, the Big Five national selectors picked 12

other wings some of whom were not wings at all. Phil Bennett, for example, made his first start for Wales on the right wing, against the Springboks at the Arms Park in January 1970. Another player capped on the wing, Ian Hall of Aberavon, would become better known by his feats for club and country as a centre.

The full list of wings reflected the recurring difficulty the selectors found during those four years from 1968 to 1972: Stuart Watkins, Keri Jones, Laurie Daniel, Maurice Richards, Andy Morgan, Stuart Ferguson, Gerald Davies, Phil Bennett, Ian Hall, Jim Shanklin, Keith Hughes, Roy Mathias, John C Bevan, not to be confused with John D Bevan, the Aberavon, Wales and Lions fly half, captain of Neath Cricket Club who died in 1986 at the age of 38.

Within two years of his one and only match for Wales, against France in April 1970, Mathias had followed Richards along the yellow brick road to the north of England. He signed for St Helens where he scored 218 tries in 412 appearances, enough to put him fifth on the Saints' all-time list headed by the South African, Tom van Vollenhoven.

Mathias had been born almost 18 months after JJ and yet his international career in Union had come and gone before his successor on the wing at Llanelli got round to starting his. The strangest aspect of JJ's career is that it took him so long to win his cap, until eight days before he had reached the ripe old age of 25.

It wasn't that the Big Five chose to keep him waiting but the player's capacity for running like the wind. Had he not spent so much time pursuing his ambition to become an international athlete, inevitably to some extent at the expense of his rugby development, there might well have been more than one John Williams on the block-busting Lions tour of New Zealand in the summer of 1971.

There is, as they say, a price for everything.

JJ

FOR AN ASPIRING athlete and teacher, Cardiff College of Education was *the* place to be in the late 1960s. As a student there, I was able to rub shoulders not just with exceptional rugby players and athletes but basketballers, footballers and gymnasts of high calibre.

Their presence gave me the chance to observe how they trained and how they behaved at close quarters. It was a priceless education. The College rugby team was so teeming with talent that at one stage they had six scrum-halves who were all playing for various first-class clubs outside College, a list headed by Gareth Edwards.

There were also numerous British and Welsh international athletes, all working in a hothouse environment created by Lynn Davies in his role as a lecturer. After what seemed like an interminable time being torn between the two sports, I finally made the decision to give up rugby in my final year at College, from September 1969.

I did so for one reason, so that I could concentrate without any distraction on making the Wales team for the Commonwealth Games of 1970 in Edinburgh. At the time, as captain of the College athletics team, I considered it the right decision. Now, in hindsight, I am not so sure.

Yes, it was a thrill to represent my country at the Commonwealth Games but at what cost? I have long suspected that if I had gone flat out on my rugby career from the word go that I would have been capped much sooner. Even now, after all these years, I still can't get rid of that suspicion.

There's no point beating myself up about it after all this time but you can't help asking yourself every once in a while: 'What if...?' In the four years before I eventually got my cap in 1973, wing positions in the Wales team were up for grabs, partly because of the retirement of people like

Stuart Watkins and the switch to rugby league of people like Maurice Richards, Roy Mathias and John Bevan.

At times Wales were so short in the wing department that they put Phil Bennett on the right wing for one game. I look back and think I could have been good enough to have played my first international at 20 or 21 and had I done that, who knows? I might even have made the 1971 Lions and been a part of the first, and only, series win over the All Blacks in New Zealand.

For the aspiring international, today's game is very different to the one I knew when I was 18 years old. Professionalism has cleared the way for the most gifted young backs to make the first team in the three big European leagues and, in exceptional cases like George North, for their country while they are still in their teens.

They leave school early and go straight into the academies run by the main professional centres – clubs in England and France, provinces in Ireland, regions in Wales and the two big city teams in Scotland. The vast majority of the academy lads spend too much time in the gym pumping iron and too little, far too little, on the pitch sharpening their skills. There is too much emphasis on size, too little on skill.

Had I been born 40 years later, in 1988 instead of 1948, maybe I would have won my Welsh cap a lot quicker than I did. Then I think of what I would have missed, the fun and camaraderie of college rugby and the opportunity to develop my game against a cross section of Welsh rugby.

Our fixture list ensured we experienced the game at different levels. Every three weeks or so we would have the privilege of testing ourselves against a first-class team like Neath or Bridgend mixed in with a string of fixtures against second-class teams.

I was in my second year and looking forward to the Christmas holiday when I suffered another family tragedy.

In the days before they built the University of Wales hospital in the Heath district of Cardiff, we stayed in barracks at Heath Park where I shared a room with Leigh Jones, the international gymnast.

We were woken up sometime between two and three o'clock in the morning so, instinctively, I knew it was bad news about something. It could not have been worse. I stood, bleary-eyed, at the door to be told that Mam had passed away. She had never enjoyed the best of health but it still came as a horrible shock to learn that she'd had a fatal heart attack.

I have always been convinced, and remain so to this day, that she died of a broken heart. My great regret is that my parents did not live to enjoy retirement and that I didn't have the business brain then that would have ensured they lived out their twilight years in comparative comfort.

They would have been bursting with pride to have seen their youngest son represent Wales at two sports and to have had a daughter-in-law as beautiful as Jane. She only met my mother on a few occasions, all before our wedding and Jane's fondest memory is of going to our terraced house for lunch.

My mother always cooked potatoes. Every meal featured a pile of chips which made sense with four growing boys to feed. Just about the last time Jane came to lunch, she told my mother that she was on a diet which ruled out potatoes. So Mam gave her chips instead. Jane was far too polite to cause a fuss and she suspended her diet, for one day only.

Potatoes had played an even bigger part of my family folklore. My paternal grandparents owned the local fish-and-chip shop in the village and when my dad's brother, uncle Tal, returned from the Second World War after being taken prisoner, he was given the job of running the business.

I have often asked my brothers why my father didn't ask for his share in the shop. There was such sympathy for uncle Tal and what he had been through for king and country that the subject was never discussed.

My mother must have been very worried by the financial pressures she had inherited after Dad's death. She was putting me through college and running out of money at the same time. While her health was never that good at the best of times, I believe the anxiety of her life as a widow contributed to her dying of a broken heart.

It was a terrible time. Losing my father was bad enough and now, two years later, I had lost my mother. With both parents gone, I felt a painful sense of loneliness. It would fill me with despair and whenever that happened, I'd end up asking myself the same question over and over again: 'What am I going to do?'

Now I had to work things out for myself and the realisation that I had nobody to turn to made me feel vulnerable. My three older brothers did everything they could but at some stage I had to learn to stand on my own two feet because, apart from anything else, they had to get on with their lives.

After Dad's death, Mam had made all sorts of sacrifices, always making sure she was there to support me in my dual role as an athlete and a rugby player. Her passing meant the house had to be sold and so another part of my childhood, one which I thought would be there forever, had gone.

By the time the money was divided between the four boys, we had about £300 each. It doesn't sound much now but in the late 1960s it was enough for me to go into Cardiff and buy my first car, a yellow Mini. While it enabled me to get around, my life would never be quite the same again but I knew I had to knuckle down and make the most of my time at College by doing something to make Mam proud.

As students we spent all day together attending lectures and very nearly all night training for the game on Saturday. Professionalism in those days meant rugby league or soccer. Rugby union was gloriously amateur and it is no exaggeration to say that the majority of those amateurs hurled themselves gloriously into the social scene bubbling around the game.

Whenever the College team played away, more often than not a bus-load of supporters would follow us, most of them mini-skirted girls taking a weekend off from their studies. The social side was huge. For the players, drinking became almost as important as playing but not for me as a budding athlete.

Out of my year, a few graduated to senior rugby, like Roger Lane who went on to establish himself at No. 8 for Cardiff. In almost ten years at the Arms Park, he built an envied reputation as an outstanding back row forward of the 1970s but to play for Wales during that Golden Era you had to be more than just outstanding.

Roger was unlucky enough to be at the peak of his game when another No. 8 was at the peak of his, Mervyn Davies. Remember, in those days Wales would play five capped internationals a season at the very most and the strictly limited use of replacements meant they weren't handing caps out then for five minutes here or ten minutes there, the way they do these days.

Ian Lewis was another of my college team-mates who suffered a similar fate. Where Roger had to contend with 'Merve', Phil Bennett's emergence at Llanelli prevented Ian from getting national recognition as one of the best fly-halves of his time. Instead he had to make do with setting Bridgend's backs alight, amongst them another College old boy, the centre Norman Lang.

Despite dropping rugby for a while, I still managed to win our main cup competition, the Silver Ball, three times and score tries galore, including six one Wednesday afternoon against Cardiff University. Roy Bish, senior lecturer at the College and also coach of Cardiff RFC, saw the game and approached me afterwards.

'You looked tired out there,' he said, which made me think

how many more I would have scored had I been a bit less tired. 'I can see that all that heavy athletics training is taking a toll. So I'll come straight to the point. Make up your mind – rugby or athletics.'

I already had. Even before then I knew it was going to be full steam ahead for the Commonwealth Games in Edinburgh in the summer of the following year, 1970. I could not have wished for better facilities than those put at my disposal by the College at Cyncoed.

Lynn Davies, a constant source of inspiration, was a certainty for gold in the long jump. Trying to find where Wales would win another medal, of any colour, was difficult to say the least.

I was never going to win one in the sprints, not when you considered the calibre of the opposition. Two sprinters from the Caribbean stood head and shoulders above us all – Don Quarrie from Jamaica who would go on to win Olympic gold, and Lennox Miller from Trinidad, a future Olympic silver medallist.

Gold for Wales in Edinburgh began and ended with 'The Leap' but we did have an excellent 4x100 relay team. We had planned it all with meticulous care. Terry Davies, a British international, was to run the first leg, Lynn Davies, a former British sprint champion, the second, I'd take care the third, and the great Ron Jones would bring us flying home over the last hundred.

We knew our place. Gold would be a two-horse race – Jamaica against Trinidad and Tobago, leaving the bronze medal up for grabs between England, Scotland and Wales. Peter Lay, then Wales' national athletics coach, had perfected our hand-overs so effectively that we shaved a few priceless hundredths of seconds off the time we took to get the baton round.

In all our races before the Games, we had beaten England

and Scotland regularly. We knew that, provided we gave Ron Jones the baton ahead of our British rivals, nobody was going to overtake him for third place. Ron was the Linford Christie of his time – the best of British and a relay specialist who a few years earlier had helped Britain beat the United States of America in a world record time at White City.

As each day passed at the Games and more of us crashed out of our individual events, so the relay assumed still more importance. I, too, crashed out but not before I'd got through a few rounds and found myself drawn in Lane 1 against the great Mr Quarrie who was settling into his blocks in Lane 2. Needless to say, there was only one winner.

At least I was free to concentrate on the relay. My girlfriend, Jane, and all my family had made the long trek up to Scotland, ensuring that if we failed, it wouldn't be for any lack of moral support. The 4x100 took place on the last day of the Games with the semi-final and final all to be run off in a matter of hours.

And then, when the big day dawned, when all our painstaking attention to detail and preparation would surely be rewarded with a place on the rostrum, disaster! Ron Jones, the ace in our pack, had dropped out. If we were going to win a medal we would have to do it without our world-beating anchor man.

I was blissfully unaware that Ron had been struggling with a serious knee injury. They gave him cortisone injections that morning but they didn't work. Ron was out and Howard Davies was in – a high-class 400-metre runner but not in the same class as Ron for sheer speed over the shorter distance.

We cruised through the semi-final, securing an excellent middle lane draw for the final. When I handed the baton over to Howard at the end of the third leg, we were in the bronze medal position behind Jamaica and Trinidad. You can imagine how we all felt when the last Scottish and English runners pipped us on the line.

We were all absolutely gutted. I don't think in all my sporting years that I ever felt as devastated as I felt that day at the Meadowbank Stadium in Edinburgh. I still can't really find the words to do justice to the overpowering sense of disappointment I felt at coming away from my one and only Commonwealth Games empty-handed. A bronze medal on my CV would have been rather nice.

Over the years since, I never fail to remind Ron of the medal that got away. I pull his leg about how his injury cost us the bronze and he takes it in good part. I have nothing but total respect for a fabulous sprinter and a fine ambassador for the sport who still has the energy to raise sponsorship for the next generation of Welsh sports stars in his role as director of SportsAid Cymru Wales. And to think he turned 80 in 2014.

They say that when one door shuts another opens and that proved to be the case for me after Edinburgh. I was still feeling down in the dumps when I was informed that I had made the Great Britain team for the World Student Games in Turin a little later that summer.

I had four weeks to prepare, long enough to ensure that I arrived in Italy in peak condition. Representing GB was a real honour, all the more so when I found out that I was the only Welsh athlete in a squad which included David Hemery, then the reigning Olympic 400-metres hurdles champion, and the middle-distance runner Brendan Foster.

As a shy Valleys boy, I felt an outsider and found mixing with the top brass of British athletics, most of whom were Oxbridge types, quite intimidating. That was the least of my worries. All too soon the Turin experience began to turn into the most miserable of my sporting life.

Within days of arriving in Italy, I went down with food poisoning. Boiling temperatures of 35 centigrade didn't help.

Neither did the shortage of available water although when family history repeated itself and my son, Rhys, went down with the same problem, at the World Student Games in İzmir, Turkey, he at least had a plentiful supply of water.

Needless to say, I ran like a novice in Turin and stumbled out of the 100 metres in the first round and then suffered the same fate in the relay. I couldn't get home quick enough and I took a long time to get over the fact that my time as an international athlete had ended on such a low note.

At least I could forget the disappointment and return to rugby knowing that it offered me the one remaining chance to make a name for myself. Before I could make a big enough impression on the Big Five that I really had what it took to be an international wing, I had the opportunity to change direction and go down an entirely different footballing route.

Swansea Harriers were my athletics club then and they got in touch to say that Harry Gregg, the manager of Swansea Town as they were known then, had asked them to put him in touch with someone who could take charge of sprint training. The next thing I knew I was at the Vetch Field meeting Harry and his assistant, Roy Saunders, whose son Dean became a top-class striker at a number of clubs, including Liverpool.

Their enthusiasm impressed me right from the outset, not that the Swans then were anything like the Premier League force they would become. The great Ivor Allchurch hadn't long retired although some of the players still at the club then were household names, like Barrie Hole, Herbie Williams and David Gwyther.

With the club on the slide in the lower divisions of the Football League, Harry took over after Roy Bentley resigned. Harry, of course, had been a famous goalkeeper for Manchester United and Northern Ireland and nobody ever dared question his courage, before or after the Munich air disaster which claimed the lives of so many of the 'Busby Babes'.

Suddenly, there I was sitting in the cramped manager's office at the Vetch talking to the man who had been acclaimed for his bravery in going back into the wreckage of the plane and rescuing some of the survivors. He wanted me to meet the players straight away and take them down to the athletics track on Sketty Road in Swansea.

So off I went and after a brief introduction we got down to business. I put the Swans' players on the same regime which I used – a 60-metre sprint with a 30-second recovery period, repeated six times. Then we did a second set with a two-minute rest at the end and finished up with a third set. Speed endurance sessions were totally alien to soccer players at that time.

I ran alongside the players and they could not believe that I could do a session like that and have enough wind to shout instructions as I ran. The session blew them away, not because they weren't fit but because it was something they had never done before.

The players hated it but Harry and the coaches loved it. Fitness sessions used by football clubs in those days were pretty much taken out of the training manual used by the Army. I also taught the players how to warm-up, showing them the proper way of stretching, striding and running drills.

Speed off the mark is a priceless asset but it has to be based on the right preparation. The improvement in the sharpness of the team as a whole was amazing. When the manager told them to run, nobody refused. If they did, they were fined on the spot and for me that was a real eye-opener, a big difference between a professional sport and an amateur one.

Then one day Harry called me into his office. 'Right son,' he said. 'We are very pleased with the work you've been doing on a part-time basis. Now we want you on board full-time as part of the coaching staff.'

Harry was way ahead of his time because nobody in the early 1970s had thought about sprint coaches in football. From the unbeatable vantage point of hindsight, I can see that thanks to Harry Gregg's foresight, I could easily have made a career for myself as the first of a new breed, the football sprints coach.

I would have made more money than I could have dreamt of and I could still have continued playing rugby, if only in my spare time. The Swans had paid me in cash for every session. Their invitation was an attractive one because the money they were paying was a lot more than I could earn as a schoolteacher. Much more!

There are always big decisions to be made at certain junctures in everyone's life. Some of those big decisions I got right, others I didn't. The Swansea Town offer was certainly one I let slip away but then it wasn't as straightforward as it appeared.

It came just as I was about to achieve my goal of qualifying as a schoolteacher. That had been the whole point of my three years at college and the Swans approach came after I had been offered a position on the staff at Hartridge High School, a very large complex spread over some 40 acres to serve a council estate in Newport. My qualification depended on completing a probationary year and it turned out to be a challenging experience.

I enjoyed it – great kids and a great staff but, from my perspective, there was one major problem with the school. They didn't have a rugby team because they had a football one. Luckily for me, the head of sport, Reg Townsend, wanted to get rugby going in a big way and that was a major reason behind my appointment.

The first rugby lesson I took during that first week in September was a real eye-opener. The first-year kids didn't have a clue about it but they embraced the sport with so much enthusiasm that by the end of the season they were winning most of their games.

I left after that first year and, as if to show that nothing stays the same, the school has since been renamed Llanwern High. The pupils who I had introduced to the game went from strength to strength and duly formed their own Old Boys' club. I'd like to think I played a small part in spreading the rugby gospel…

CHAPTER 3
Scarlet Fever

Peter Jackson

THE EARLY 1970s produced some performances so astounding that they are still talked of today. The Lions won a Test series in New Zealand for the first and only time. A Belgian grocer's son, Eddy Merckx, won the Tour de France, arguably sport's most gruelling endurance test, four times in a row.

Americans still tended to monopolise the major tournaments in golf and tennis. US golfers hogged the Open Championship (Lee Trevino in 1971 and 1972, Jack Nicklaus in 1973), the Masters (Charles Coody 1971, Nicklaus 1972, Tommy Aaron 1973), the US Open (Trevino 1971, Nicklaus 1972, Johnny Miller 1973) and the US PGA (Nicklaus 1971, 1973). Only Gary Player broke the American sequence during those years, the South African winning the US PGA at Oakland Hills in 1972.

Stan Smith won the Wimbledon men's singles for Uncle Sam that same year and Billie Jean King won the women's. At the summer Olympics in Munich, another American announced himself as one of the most phenomenal Olympians of all time, the swimmer Mark Spitz.

He had won two golds, a silver and bronze in Mexico four years earlier, an almost feeble effort compared to Munich. There Spitz won seven golds, in the 100-metre freestyle, the 100-metre butterfly, the 200-metre freestyle, the 200-metre butterfly, the 4x100-metre medley relay, the 4x100-metre freestyle and the 4x200-metre freestyle.

As if that wasn't astounding enough, he broke the world record in each and every swim. The Californian reduced the Male Athlete of the Year award to the most foregone of conclusions. An elf-like Russian gymnast had a similar effect on the Female Athlete of the Year – Olga Korbut.

That same summer saw a Welsh-based Scottish boxer make the long haul from Merthyr Tydfil to New York in pursuit of a world title. Ken Buchanan, then managed by the incomparable Eddie Thomas, made the trip undaunted at challenging one of the all-time greats, Roberto Durán.

The Panamanian whose predilection for knocking opponents out earned him the nickname 'Hands of Stone', stopped Buchanan in the 13th round at Madison Square Garden in June 1971, winning the world lightweight title for the first time. He held it for nine years until Sugar Ray Leonard put an end to his reign at which point Durán went up a weight to take the world welterweight crown, then up another to rule the middleweight roost before retiring at 50.

The advent of the 1970s coincided with the first one-day cricket international (Australia v England in Melbourne), as well as the first of three colossal duels between Muhammad Ali and Joe Frazier for the world heavyweight title. History has long acknowledged it with typically pugilistic hyperbole as 'The Fight of the Century'.

The decade also began the way the previous one had finished as far as the Ryder Cup was concerned, with the USA beating the best of British and Irish in America easily enough. That was hardly a surprise given that the holders' line-up included Nicklaus, Trevino and Arnold Palmer.

Back on this side of the Atlantic, Wales won the Grand Slam, Mill Reef the Derby and L'Escargot the Cheltenham Gold Cup. While all that was happening, a newly-qualified, newly-married schoolteacher would soon play his part in ensuring that the tectonic plates underpinning the pecking order of world rugby took a seismic shift...

JJ

BRIDGEND WON THE last Welsh club championship of the 1960s and the first of the 1970s. When Wales achieved the Grand Slam in 1971 they did it without picking a single player from what could reasonably have been described as the best club team in the country.

Fair play to the Big Five, they did get round to picking one Bridgend player for the Five Nations in 1972. John Dawes' retirement meant they had to find a new captain and John Lloyd, Bridgend's loosehead prop, got the job, deservedly so. He was the only one from Bridgend.

I kept asking myself: 'How come? Why was every player, bar one, of what was then the most consistent club side in Wales over three seasons, being ignored by the national selectors?'

The more I thought about it, the more I began to suspect that we had become victims of something which has never been too far beneath the surface of the game in Wales – politics.

The late Ivor John ran the Bridgend club almost single-handedly. A manager in the British Steel Corporation, he was Mr Bridgend and I always had a sneaking suspicion that Bridgend were not getting the Welsh representation they deserved because Ivor had upset one of the selectors.

Ivor was a great man for Bridgend and a great supporter of mine. He was bitterly disappointed when I left but, as time went by, he realised that I had made the right decision. It must have hurt him that Wales picked so few Bridgend players during a period when they were the best team in the country.

The second time we won the title, in 1969–70, I scored 33 tries at the rate of one a game. There were times when I wondered what more I had to do to get some sort of recognition from the Big Five, and the fact that I had sacrificed what was left of my athletics career to give rugby a serious shot really tested my patience.

I wasn't kidding myself that I was worth a place in the Wales team but I thought I was worthy of playing for Wales B. The whole point of having a second-string team was to try out up-and-coming youngsters at a level higher than the club game but still a long way below the intensity of a full international.

After the anticlimax of the Commonwealth Games and the World Student Games, I kept running for one more season, throughout the summer of 1971. By then I moved from the sprints to quarter-miling, the 400 metres and did a career-best for the distance of sub-47 seconds which is shifting by anyone's yardstick.

I was still involved with Swansea Harriers and remember one particularly hectic weekend. I played in a sevens' invitational tournament at Newport on the Saturday and on the Sunday rushed off to London to run for the Harriers in a British League match in west London where I won the 100 metres, the 200 and had a hand in the club winning both relays, the 4x100 and 4x400. In doing so, I made a massive contribution towards Swansea Harriers gaining British League status in 1971.

My life was changing and changing rapidly. After my probationary year at Hartridge High School, I had become head of physical education at my old school, Maesteg Comprehensive, at the ripe old age of 23 which must have made me the youngest departmental head in Welsh education at the time.

It was a dream appointment. I was welcomed back with

open arms by the staff, some of whom had taught me. I would spend the next four years at Maesteg Comprehensive and I can say, hand on heart, that I loved every minute of it.

My main function was to inject some life into the PE department, especially on the rugby field which was right up my street. My old PE master, Mr David Brown, was still there, in a different capacity as a careers' teacher but he was always on hand to give me advice whenever I needed it.

During my first year the intention was to strengthen the first XV to be more competitive in the Welsh schools' arena. To do that you need the raw material and it was fair to say that I realised soon enough that my expectation exceeded the team's overall ability.

We had some great lads but there was no escaping the fact that I was struggling to galvanise them into a decent team. Strength in depth had been a big problem at the start but by the end of my third year we were putting out a second and third XV in addition to the main team every Saturday morning.

I made no apology for spreading the rugby gospel at every opportunity. Every boy who came into the gym had a serious work-out which was always based on a rugby theme. My bias towards the sport would have had me in trouble by today's standards and while it was rugby, rugby and more rugby, I can say without fear of contradiction that the boys thrived on it.

A few went on to achieve great things in the game. Gwyn Evans, for example, played full back for Maesteg, Wales and the 1983 Lions, following in my footsteps all the way to New Zealand in 1983. Rhodri Lewis and Mark Davies were both capped by Wales in the back row, Leighton O'Connor and David Arthur played for Wales B.

David was the most talented one of all, a real stalwart of the school. Had I stayed longer and therefore been able to have a closer influence on his later years, I think he would have won many caps for Wales as a second row forward.

I hadn't completed my first year when a far more important event took place. Jane and I got married during the Easter holiday in April 1972. In terms of planning for the big day, weddings now involve meticulous organising and I speak from some experience having been involved in the arrangements for the marriage of our three children.

Compared to that, I look back on my big day with some embarrassment. All I did (apart from turn up at the church on time!) was to ask my brother Peter to be my best man. I didn't even arrange my honeymoon. I left that to one of my other brothers, Ken and, typically, he forgot to tick the box on the booking form to say we were on honeymoon.

As a consequence, Jane never got her champagne and flowers on arrival at our hotel in Majorca. That was bad enough. Unfortunately, another couple of newlyweds from Bridgend were also staying at the same hotel and they kept going on about the champagne and flowers they were given on arrival and that made my family's oversight twice as bad.

Needless to say, Jane does remind me about it from time to time which is why I've been trying to make it up to her ever since. The only other tricky part of a rugby player being married on Easter Monday is to avoid a clash of fixtures which, in my case, meant missing the most important match of the season – the local derby, Bridgend versus Maesteg.

I was under strict orders not to play the week before the wedding. I was gutted at missing the local derby but orders are orders and the last thing Jane wanted was to see her hubby limping down the aisle with a black eye. I compromised and played on Good Friday instead, against London Irish and helped myself to a hat-trick.

The second order from Jane dictated that Peter and I arrive at her mother's friend's house a full two hours before the wedding. Punctuality has never been my strongest point and Jane was taking no chances even if it meant two of the Williams' boys were left to kick their heels.

We were married at Llangunnor Church, Jane's family church perched in a wonderful location at the top of a hill overlooking the Towy Valley outside Carmarthen. Somebody up there had arranged the weather for us. It was a beautiful spring day, Jane looked amazing, and I had the privilege of joining a new family.

Jane's parents, Ralph and Mary, were a lovely couple. My only regret was that my parents had not lived to see the day and, in some respects, Ralph and Mary filled part of the void. Once I'd joined Llanelli, I spent even more time with my in-laws and that could have had a detrimental effect on my speed as a wing.

Mary's cooking was so exceptional that I needed all my self-discipline to stop her spoiling me too much. Ralph became a patron of Llanelli RFC and always brought his own brand of passionate support to the Scarlets' cause.

Within a week or so of returning from our honeymoon in Majorca, I went off with Bridgend to Canada for three weeks and we spent all the time based in British Columbia. It gave Jane an early sample of what married life would be like in those years but she was brilliant in the way she coped then and has been brilliant ever since.

Our presence in their midst might not have captured the imagination of the Canadian nation as a whole but they made a big fuss of us in B.C. as the first Wales team to play there. They went to a lot of trouble to use the biggest stadia available and were delighted when a couple of thousand turned up for some of the matches.

The Canadians then were making huge strides towards becoming a force strong enough to qualify for World Cups, not that the tournament had been invented in the early 1970s.

They also had a heavy Welsh influence, one of whom was a former Aberavon player by the name of Alan Rees. His son, Gareth, would become the first 18 year old to appear in an English Cup final, for Wasps, and go on to establish himself as a top-class goal-kicking outside half.

It would be fair to assume that the Rees family knew rather more about rugby union than some of the Canadian journalists. They gave me a few headlines and the excuse to introduce me with a nickname, 'The Blur', inspired after I'd scored four in one game.

The tour also enabled me to renew my rivalry with an opposition wing then busy making a name for himself as the most colourful rugby player in the whole of North America, Mr Spence McTavish. He had long, blond hair which he tied back in a very fetching headband. He looked more like an Apache warrior than a rugby player.

We had been in direct opposition twice on successive weekends the previous season. Canada made their first tour of Wales and after beating a Monmouthshire under-25 team at Rodney Parade and Western Counties at Stradey Park, they played Wales B at Swansea on the last Saturday of September 1971.

McTavish and I marked each other that day at St Helen's and while I got one try, the other wing, Jeff Davies of Swansea, got three. We won 38–10, which was rough on McTavish because he was a real handful. We met again one week later at Cardiff Arms Park – Wales versus Canada, a full international in every sense except that no caps were awarded.

The Welsh Rugby Union had a policy of giving caps only against those countries who had been founder-members of the International Rugby Board. Apart from anything else, it belittled emerging rugby nations like Canada, as if they were saying: 'We'll give you a game but our boys won't get caps because we don't think you're good enough.'

How times have changed. Not only are caps now given against all national opposition, and rightly so, they have been chucked about on recent occasions for matches against the Barbarians which is absolutely nonsense. A club team elevated to Test-match status? The WRU didn't just do it once, in June 2011, they did again 12 months later.

Anyway, we beat Canada ten to two on tries, 56–10 on points. The other Welsh wing that day, Roy Mathias of Llanelli, got a hat-trick, I drew a blank and guess who got both Canada's tries? Spence McTavish. For me the trickiest part of an otherwise enjoyable occasion came after the referee, Alan Hosie of Scotland, had blown for full-time.

McTavish took off his jersey and handed it towards me, expecting mine in return. He was very keen to do a swop. I wasn't. I treasured that first Welsh jersey and having waited so long for the honour of wearing it made me treasure it all the more. The replica jersey was unheard of in those days. The only way you could wear a Wales jersey was by being picked to play in one, not nipping off to the nearest sports shop to buy your own.

I was still fighting my corner, so to speak, but not for much longer. Here was this big bear of a man with his long blond hair tied in a bandana expecting me to hand it over without further delay. He wasn't taking no for an answer.

'Spence I'm sorry,' I tried to tell him. 'This is my first and I want to keep it.'

He kept persisting. 'Come on John,' he said in that Canadian drawl. 'I've gotta have it.'

And he kept on until I gave in. I was keen to avoid creating any impression of being at all unfriendly so I gave him the jersey. I took Spence's jersey and handed it on to Nantyffyllon Rugby Club, not that they were overly-impressed. They thought they'd be getting my Welsh one. I'd have to wait for the return trip to Canada at the end of the season to get another.

Before he flew back home, Spence made me a promise. 'John,' he says. 'When you touch down in our country next May, I'll be at the airport to meet you.'

What I wanted more than anything was to win my cap. I knew John Bevan and Gerald Davies were in my way and that I would have to bide my time. But first of all I had to get into the national squad and that was proving difficult, very difficult.

After returning from Vancouver with Bridgend in the summer of 1972, my first instinct was to carry on as I'd done before and spend the close season on the running track. A full academic year as head of department in a large comprehensive and a long season with Bridgend made longer by the transatlantic tour had left me exhausted, not that I realised it at the time.

Jane and I were living in a little flat in Ogmore-by-sea, settling into married life and enjoying the summer holidays. One evening I went sprint training as normal at RAF St Athan and, halfway through the session, the penny dropped. It dawned on me that my priorities were no longer in athletics. Even though I had entered the Welsh Championships and the Taff Street Dash in Pontypridd, I knew that my heart wasn't in it any longer.

I ran a few more races for my club, Swansea Harriers, by which time my career in athletics had just about run its course, even if I was only 24. Sometimes I look back and wonder how good I could have been. My future would have been as a 400-metre runner with a personal best sub-47 seconds which would have put me a long way up the British rankings. The Welsh record, held by Howard Davies, wasn't far out of my reach at 46.6.

Two facts are beyond dispute: one, I wasn't in the same class as the Americans and, two, I would never have achieved on the track what I subsequently achieved on the rugby field.

Getting picked for the Canadian tour at the end of the 1972–3 season meant that I had a foot on the ladder but they kept me waiting. When they named the national squad shortly after the start of the following season in September 1972, my name was nowhere to be seen.

I was in my 25th year and my representative appearances at that stage could be counted not so much on the fingers of one hand but on one finger! The previous season, in October 1971, I had played for Wales in the annual B fixture against France in the old Stade Colombes, although 'played' might have been an exaggeration.

We were outplayed to such an extent that I didn't touch the ball. Neither did my fellow international sprinter, Terry Davies of London Welsh, on the opposite wing. The French scrum half, Jean-Michel Aguirre, later to star for his country at full back, ran the match as though he had the ball on a string and they walloped us 30–9. I went back to Bridgend as if nothing had happened and that was the problem – nothing had happened.

For whatever reason, I wasn't being recognised and while I was still trying to find out why, I played for Bridgend against Llanelli at Stradey Park. We thought we were good but they tore us to shreds with a dazzling exhibition of 15-man rugby.

They overran us from start to finish. I spent what seemed to be the entire match out on the right wing trying to cope with a never-ending wave of overlaps coming at me. Llanelli had just begun their centenary season and they were very excited about a special match in a few weeks' time at the end of October, against the All Blacks.

On the way back home, I realised that if I was ever going to be an international rugby player I would have to be scoring tries for a team at the very top of their game. The runaround we had that night at Stradey left me feeling very disgruntled and totally frustrated at my lack of progress.

I decided to do something about it. I was quite friendly with Ray 'Chico' Hopkins, the scrum half who had transferred from Maesteg to Llanelli the year before and made such an impression that he was picked for the Lions tour of New Zealand that summer. Tommy David had moved from Pontypridd to Llanelli at the same time as 'Chico'.

They had been approached by Carwyn James in his capacity as the Scarlets' coach about joining the club. I hadn't had any such invitation and while I was still in a dissatisfied state of mind, I watched Llanelli play Neath in a televised match which showed Welsh club rugby in all its glory – fabulous rugby played in front of an enormous crowd.

I sat on the sofa thinking to myself: 'I'd love to be a part of that.' At last, I decided to take the bull by the horns. If Carwyn wasn't going to invite me, then maybe I should invite myself, so I asked 'Chico' to ask Carwyn if I would be at all welcome at Stradey.

Quite by chance, my approach could not have come at a more opportune time. Roy Mathias, who had been capped by Wales, had cashed in his Union chips and gone north to play rugby league for St Helens. It left a vacancy which I was desperately keen to fill.

Anyway, 'Chico' came back and told me: 'Carwyn would be pleased to meet you. He wants you to come down to his house on Sunday night after he gets home from chapel and have a chat.'

As a deacon, chapel was an important part of Carwyn's life. I waited until he'd had plenty of time to get back home and then knocked on the door of his bungalow in the village of Cefneithin. I was surprised to find that the chairman of Llanelli, Handel Greville, was there waiting to greet me with Carwyn.

I said: 'Mr James, I would like to come and join Llanelli.' And he said: 'Of course. We would be pleased to have you and we would like you to play against Swansea this coming Saturday.'

That the best coach in the world, which is what he was then, thought I was good enough to jump into the best club side in the British Isles did wonders for my self-belief. I'd been prepared to plead for a chance, if necessary, and here was Carwyn James telling me I'd be going straight into his team.

That was the easy bit. Transferring from one club to another in an amateur sport like rugby union ought to have been a simple matter. Instead, it proved to be such a complicated business that it must have been easier for Gareth Bale when he moved from Spurs to Real Madrid.

Bridgend were very annoyed when I told them I was moving on, which was a crying shame because I thought I'd given them good service (99 tries in 100 matches). Instead of letting me go with their best wishes, they insisted that I could only play for Llanelli on permit and then just for six games. That meant taking a letter from the club to the secretary of the Welsh Rugby Union, Bill Clement, at the Union's headquarters in central Cardiff.

I had to rush from school late on the Friday afternoon and collect the permit from the Union before their offices closed at 5.30p.m. That went on every week for six weeks and on more than one occasion Norman Gale, the forwards' coach at Llanelli, would drive east from his home, I'd head west from mine, and we'd meet halfway in Port Talbot so he could take delivery of the precious permit.

Bridgend were still very miffed about my departure from the Brewery Field. It came at a time when someone at the club was helping me secure the purchase of my first house in Bridgend for £4,500. Negotiations were well advanced but after I let it be known that I was going to join Llanelli, the price of the property suddenly shot up to £7,500.

That gave some idea of how sore some people connected

with Bridgend Rugby Club were over my move. Others accused me of making money. Money? Llanelli paid me enough to cover my petrol expenses but nothing more. Far from making money, I lost stacks of it in being gazumped £2,500 in the property market – the equivalent of over £50,000 on 2015 prices.

Even without that, I was making a massive sacrifice to further my career at Llanelli. The M4 didn't stretch that far west in those days which meant I would leave Maesteg as soon as school finished and drive to Stradey for training twice a week. Sometimes Tommy David and I would travel down together, Tommy coming from his home in Pontypridd, some 20 miles further east.

The petrol money I received in expenses just about covered my costs but that didn't bother me in the slightest. I wanted to find out how far I could go in rugby, whether I could hack it at the highest level and if there was a price to be paid for achieving that, I was more than happy to pay it.

Llanelli had a magnetic appeal which I couldn't resist. I loved the stylish way they played the game but what I didn't know until I got there was that their indoor training and medical facilities were way ahead of their time. Although 'Chico' and Tommy were the only players I knew, I struck up a relationship straight away with Phil Bennett, Ray Gravell and the rest.

I trained with them twice during that first week and that was a real eye-opener in terms of the quality of players they had who weren't able to get into the first team – like Gwyn Ashby, Lyn Davies, Bernard Thomas and Alan Lewis who had the misfortune to break his leg badly during a match against Swansea. But for that, Alan would have unquestionably made it to the very top.

I was taken aback by their collective skills. Everyone gave me a friendly welcome and Carwyn was brilliant, as always, but I was on edge. I had to prove myself and as the Swansea match got ever closer, the more I became astounded at the depth of the rivalry between the clubs.

For the 'Turks', beating the Swansea 'Jacks' used to be the biggest scalp in the domestic season until all that changed with the creation of the four regional teams. For my own peace of mind, I had to do something to justify the faith which Carwyn and the others had put in me.

The bigger the occasion, the more I enjoyed it. In Welsh club terms, Swansea-Llanelli was as big as it got, two of the oldest tribes in the game going at it hammer-and-tongs. I've usually been in a rush throughout my life and it took me about five minutes to score my first try for my new club, sprinting over from the best part of 40 metres.

Shortly afterwards, I got another chance to play for Wales B against France, at Cardiff Arms Park, and this time I played instead of watched as I had done 12 months before in Paris. Tommy David captained the team and we gave the French a bigger beating than they had given us the previous year.

Tommy got two of our five tries and I managed to get one, a real stunner if I may say so. I broke down the middle, chipped over the last man and scored from the best part of 50 metres. I felt I was making progress but I had no time to dwell on it, not with a much bigger occasion looming which would hit the rugby world like a thunderbolt just ten days later.

Carwyn had an almost God-like status at Stradey. Everyone revered him, all the more so because of what he had accomplished as coach of the Lions in New Zealand the year before, winning a Test series against the All Blacks for the one and only time.

Before I met him at his home on that Sunday evening, Carwyn was already devising a plot plan to show that what he achieved in New Zealand was no flash in the pan. A man far ahead of his time, he delegated responsibility to specialist coaches, like Tom Hudson who came from Bath, to pioneer a revolution in the fitness of Welsh rugby players.

Before I went west from Bridgend, Tom had taken the Llanelli squad to a boot camp in Brecon as the base for some gruelling, stamina-building runs on the Beacons. By the time they finished climbing the mountains, they were in the ideal physical condition to climb the one that mattered most, against the All Blacks.

Tom had an uncanny knack of getting the team to peak at the most important time, so it was no coincidence that the Llanelli team of the early-to-mid 1970s won all the big games. Like a kettle on the boil, Tom was always overflowing with enthusiasm and as a leader of his field he was the first to start a sports science course at the University of Bath. He may not have had that deep a knowledge of rugby itself but Llanelli were very lucky to have had his expertise in fitness and conditioning.

Some people accused me of joining Llanelli because of that game, because it gave me a platform to show the Welsh selectors what I could do in the biggest fixture below Test level. How ridiculous. I joined Llanelli because I wanted to improve my game over a long period.

The club demanded the very best from players and in return they put us up in the very best hotels. We were treated to Sunday lunches with our wives, all on the club. Whenever the treasurer questioned the expense, Carwyn dismissed him with a wave of the hand. Whenever the treasurer kept questioning the expense, Carwyn would tell him: 'Don't worry, it's no big deal. Think of the bigger picture.'

Carwyn had charisma by the bucketful. He was a master people-person, remarkably intelligent and immaculately turned out. I was in awe of him right from the start but thrilled to find out that I was everything he wanted in a match-winning wing.

He liked the way I played the game, with an instinctive flair. The game plan at Stradey revolved around getting the ball into my hands on one wing and Andy Hill's on the other. Andy scored tries in such profusion for Llanelli that he was the first to score 300 tries for the club and you can bet your bottom dollar that he will also be the last.

Training sessions were sharp and intense. Carwyn could not have had a player better equipped to be his on-field general than Delme Thomas, a second row forward who had seen it all during two Lions tours of New Zealand. Delme's philosophy of spreading the ball as wide as possible as often as possible was music to my ears.

As well as Hudson, Carwyn was lucky to have another specialist coach in Norman Gale. If Carwyn was the magician, always striving for new ways to bamboozle the opposition with a bit of sorcery, Norman was the hard-headed pragmatist. After a lifetime in the front row, he was the perfect man to give the team its hard edge.

A steelworker by trade, he was a no-nonsense guy who knew the game inside out. His job was to ensure that the pack had the grunt and the bloody-mindedness to ensure the backs got enough of the ball to finish the job. Carwyn had complete faith in Norman and they, in turn, had complete faith in Delme.

All the preparation had to be fitted in around my professional duties as a schoolteacher and the on-going issue over house-hunting. After the Bridgend gazumping, Jane and I rented a flat in Port Talbot as a temporary measure.

We could ill afford to lose any money and, as luck would have it, the All Black match cost me a whole week's pay even though it was played during half-term. I had been invited to take an athletics' training course at Ogmore School that week.

I had to ask permission for the Tuesday off and while I

intended to go in on the Wednesday, the ecstatic aftermath of the All Black match made that a physical impossibility. So in the end I was docked a whole week's pay, not far short of £50 which in 1972 was an awful lot more than it is today.

On the Saturday before the big day, Carwyn took us all off by bus to Gloucester where the New Zealanders were playing Western Counties at the start of their tour, a 30-match trip round the British Isles and France. It would be the last of the long, traditional tours which the Kiwis had been making since 'The Originals' first came to these shores in 1905.

The All Blacks always expect to win and if, from time to time, their grim demeanour didn't exactly endear them to everyone, they didn't give two hoots. They were here to win matches, not friends and Ian Kirkpatrick's team had every reason to be in a grim mood when they began their four-month tour on the last Saturday of October 1972.

Their opponents, Western Counties, were effectively a combination of Bristol and Gloucester. A current Lion (John Pullin) and a future one (Mike Burton) were in the front row, Dave Watt of Bristol captained them from the second row and the back row included John Watkins of Gloucester and England.

The All Blacks beat them seven to one on tries with a hat-trick from Bryan 'Bee Gee' Williams on the right wing and two more from Grant Batty on the left. They won 39–12, a decent margin by anyone's standard and their performance earned them a lot of praise.

We were not exactly quaking in our boots. There was a spring in our step as we climbed back on the bus for the journey home. Carwyn caught the mood, as usual, and summed it up in one short sentence: 'These boys are beatable.'

We stopped at a restaurant near Chepstow and you could almost feel the growing sense of anticipation that we might be on to something truly historic. We trained on the Sunday and met up at the Ashburnham Hotel on the Tuesday morning, the last day of October for what would be the Halloween of our lives.

After parking the car, I walked into the hotel and saw some of the biggest hitters in the Welsh game. Ray Williams, then the world's first professional rugby coaching organiser, was there along with the Wales coach, Clive Rowlands. The WRU president said something about it being the proudest day of our lives and wished us luck.

Then Delme got down to the serious business of telling us what this game meant, not so much to ourselves but to the club and the town. His passion made a deep impression on me because I'd never heard anything like it. Remember, I was still a relative outsider. Delme's words made me realise that this was the biggest deal of the lot.

He hammered home one point above the rest, that the people of Llanelli and those of the surrounding area had lived their lives for this day – not to play the great All Blacks but to beat them. I have seen people in similar circumstances who have been unable to control their aggression. Delme kept a level head and spoke softly, all of which made what he said all the more meaningful.

Carwyn was calmness personified, the dulcet tones of his Welsh chapel voice in contrast to Norman Gale banging the drum to fire up the pack. Everyone knew what he had to do to execute our plan of spreading it wide. As it transpired, we were not allowed to play the rugby we wanted which made our victory all the greater.

Usually the big touring teams like to use the first two matches to give all 30 players a run. Surprisingly, 11 of the team that started at Gloucester started again at Stradey, including the likes of Kirkpatrick, 'Bee Gee' Williams, Joe Karam and the powerful tighthead Keith Murdoch.

It was as if they had decided not to take any chances.

Maybe they looked at our team and saw 'Chico' Hopkins at scrum half and Delme in the second row alongside Derek Quinnell. Maybe their names stirred some haunting memories because all three had played their part in the series victory achieved by the Lions the previous year.

The Ashburnham Hotel was a 20-minute drive to Stradey at the most. What awaited us as we approached Llanelli was a sight which none of us has ever forgotten. The whole town seemed to have come to a standstill. Thousands lined the streets, waving and cheering. How could we possibly let them down?

We got to Stradey before the All Blacks. We were sitting calmly in the dressing room when someone said they had arrived. A couple of us stood on a bench and looked out of the narrow window just beneath the ceiling. They stepped off the bus, some were wearing black berets which made them look all the more menacing.

I didn't say anything but I thought to myself: My God, they're mean-looking buggers. But then I shouldn't have been surprised because they played a mean game and they played it meaner than anyone else. They'd stick the ball up in the air and when it came down they'd trample over anyone standing in their way. They set out to intimidate opponents and the black berets were part of that strategy.

It was as if they were trying to send out a message of impending doom. The weather seemed to reflect their mood, grey and sombre. They were still in the course of feeling their way round Stradey when we did something which made their mood a whole lot greyer and more sombre.

Phil Bennett missed a penalty and Roy Bergiers took full advantage to ensure that we made it worth six points instead of three. When Phil's kick came back off the crossbar, their scrum half, Lyn Colling, went to clear and that was when Roy made the charge-down of his life. As the ball bounced in-goal, Roy reacted quicker than any New Zealander and dived on it for the only try of the match.

Although he went on to play for Wales and the Lions, that was surely the greatest moment of his career. Andy Hill kicked a penalty on the stroke of half-time and it was 9–0.

We went into a huddle and the All Blacks went into theirs. We knew we were 40 minutes away from history but we also knew that it we would be the toughest, longest 40 minutes we'd ever experienced. Delme said: 'We've got 'em.' Derek and 'Chico' were going round geeing everyone up, bawling out the message that everyone had to keep putting their bodies on the line.

I hadn't done much because there hadn't been anything much for me to do but all that changed when the Blacks sliced us open for the one and only time. Karam came into the line from full back and sent Grant Batty away. He chipped towards the line but I managed to use my speed to get there before him and minor the ball.

The crisis had been averted although they should have scored. Carwyn said afterwards that I had gone some way to saving the match because he reckoned that a try then would have done such wonders for the All Blacks' morale that they could have gone on to win. As it turned out, they never got another sniff because people like Delme and Derek had the game of their lives.

Our forwards got an early grip and never let it go. The All Black plan was to attack us at the tail of the line-out and use that as the platform to unleash their backs. Two players did most to scupper that – Quinnell and the No. 8 Hefin Jenkins.

Karam did land a penalty but in the grand scheme of things it didn't matter. Instead of winning 9–0 we won 9–3. At the end, Stradey went crazy and about 12 hours later, around four o'clock the next morning, the whole town was still going crazy.

Everybody but everybody seemed to be on the field at the end. My brother Terry, not what you would call a dyed-in-the-wool rugby man, was among those sweeping Delme off his feet and carrying him shoulder-high. I thought to myself: How did Terry get there?

Then I shot off in a sprint for the tunnel. The dressing room was such a heaving mass of humanity that you could hardly move. The only person I didn't see there was the one who had planned the whole thing, Carwyn James. He was never one to seek the limelight or claim his share of the glory. That didn't interest him.

In the immediate aftermath of our victory over New Zealand, he deliberately ducked out of the limelight and found a quiet corner so that he could sip a gin and tonic and have a cigarette. He was smoking away with the contented look of a man who knew the job had been done and done in a way which ensured that it would still be talked about in 50 years' time.

That was one way of escaping the shower of champagne which followed us from the dressing room upstairs at Stradey to the after-match function and then off to the main nightclub in town, the Glen Ballroom.

They used to get a lot of the top bands there in those days, like Lindisfarne, Slade and Gerry and the Pacemakers. We never thought we'd live to see the day when we would go the Glen not as a bunch of punters but as top of the bill. I wasn't a drinking man but I did have a few beers that night.

As luck would have it, I bumped into Sid Going in the toilet. He didn't like losing at the best of times, never mind to a club team and a Welsh club team at that. I felt I had to say something. It would have been rude not to, although he didn't know me.

'How are you feeling after that?' I asked, although I can see now that it was a pretty stupid question.

He fixed me with a cold stare and just said two words: 'Piss off.'

The celebrations went on all night. Jane drove me back to the Ashburnham and I never did get up in time to go back to the teaching course the next morning. I got down to sweating the beer out of my system on the Thursday and making sure I was fit for Saturday and the next match, Richmond in London.

We travelled by train and Phil Bennett slept all the way to Paddington. It was no wonder because he lived in Llanelli and everyone there wanted a piece of him which meant they were setting up drinks for him for the rest of that week. We got a bus at Paddington and as soon as 'Benny' got on board, he went back to sleep. He woke up just in time for the warm-up.

Needless to say, we lost. From that day on for the whole of that season, we were the stars of the show wherever we went. It was as if we had become the Manchester United of rugby. Beating the All Blacks had done wonders for our box-office appeal, no surprise, really, when you think of such a brilliant cast.

Delme, the line-out colossus who gave the brilliant Phil Bennett the ammunition he needed to call the shots, was surrounded by fellow Lions like Derek Quinnell and Tommy David. They would be the first to acknowledge the priceless part played by the unsung heroes, men like Tony Crocker, Roy Thomas, Gareth Jenkins, Hefin Jenkins and the brilliant Barry Llewelyn.

We had 'Chico' and Selwyn Williams at scrum, General Bennett at outside half and a pair of centres, Roy Bergiers and Ray Gravell, who were a dream to play outside. Who's to say that had Roy not broken his leg badly at the height of his career that he would have stolen quite a few headlines from 'Grav'.

One of the factors that made Llanelli so special then was

the conveyor belt of talent. Roy's midfield successor, Peter Morgan, was another example, a player of many talents who became a Lion in South Africa in 1980. I can vouch for the fact that it was a pleasure to play outside him even if I couldn't understand a word he spoke in his Pembrokeshire dialect.

On my opposite wing we had a scoring machine, the one and only Andy Hill. He didn't just score tries by the hundred but kicked long-range goals and in the summer when there weren't any tries to be scored or goals to be kicked, he competed with me as a sprinter for Swansea Harries in the British Athletics League.

At full back against the All Blacks was Roger Davies, Carwyn's dream player because he was always prepared to do something unexpected. I never understood why Roger left Llanelli after that marvellous centenary season. As one classy full back left so another arrived, Clive Griffiths.

I always wanted to take the ball when I was running flat out and not many full backs had the pace to do that. Clive did and, like Liam Williams of the current Wales team, he could easily have been capped on the wing. Shortly after his debut, as a substitute for JPR during the Triple Crown clincher against England at Cardiff in March 1979, Clive decided to take the money and embark on a successful career in rugby league.

All those big names made us ripe every once in a while for a giant-killing. We played Rhymney away in the Welsh Cup a couple of months after beating New Zealand and there must have been 5,000 there which was almost the entire population of the town. It was also very nearly an embarrassment because if it hadn't been for Andy Hill's late try, Rhymney would have beaten the team who beat the All Blacks.

It is impossible even now to overstate the role that Carwyn James played in transforming a top Welsh club into a world-class one. His reign was a comparatively brief one, long enough to set standards which he expected the players to attain every time they played. Life at Stradey would never be quite the same again.

Where he was lucky was having a lot of outstanding performers then at the peaks of their careers. Some, like Delme Thomas and Barry Llewelyn, finished a year later. 'Chico' Hopkins went to rugby league and Tommy David eventually went back to Pontypridd. They did so secure in the knowledge that history had been made and they had played their part in making it.

Every game after 31 October assumed a special significance. The rugby community throughout Britain was beginning to take serious notice of us. We were *the* team and I loved being a part of it, not least because now the Welsh selectors were taking real notice of what I could do.

Being alongside players of a different calibre raised my game. They were all outstanding and I was the one scoring the tries, largely because Phil and I were making the most of a unique rapport.

Every time he went off at a tangent, I'd go after him. Every time he made a break, I'd make it my business to be there to keep the move going. What made that Llanelli team special was the brand of rugby they played, as orchestrated by Carwyn, the supreme conductor.

The 1973 Welsh Cup final against Cardiff at the Arms Park was a classic example.

Llanelli had struggled up front 12 months earlier in the first final and lost to Neath. Plenty of experts reckoned that the Cardiff pack would take ours to the cleaners and so give Gareth Edwards an armchair ride at scrum half. Once again, Tom Hudson ensured that we went into the last match of the season in perfect physical shape. Once again, Carwyn saw to it that we were in perfect mental shape.

The result was one of the most one-sided of all finals. We took Cardiff on in the scrums, outplayed them in every aspect of the game and ran away with it, 30–7 on points, five to one on tries. I got one of my best tries that day, sidestepping off my right foot, which didn't happen that often although in my defence I could claim that was because I spent so much time on the left wing.

Forty-eight hours after Delme took the Cup home, we beat Swansea at Stradey to win another trophy, the Welsh Floodlit Alliance. And then it was back to the Arms Park for the Snelling Sevens, a big event in those days, to make it three in a row.

No club could ever have had a more magical centenary season than Llanelli in 1972–73. Wales, by comparison, looked stifled and stilted. I knew I was ready for Test football. If only someone would give me the chance...

CHAPTER 4

Drinking for Wales

NEW YEAR 1973 dawned with new promise that I might not have to wait much longer to achieve my most elusive goal. I had made the Wales squad for the first time but there were still two formidable obstacles standing between me and my cap, one very small, the other very large.

Gerald Davies, slight of stature but a master of his craft, occupied the right wing; John Bevan, a physical powerhouse from Tylorstown in the Rhondda, ruled the roost on the left and defied anyone to take it away from him. I was next in line, the No. 1 contender and the selection of the teams for the final Welsh trial at Pontypool Park on the first Saturday of the year confirmed my position in the pecking order.

Gerald and 'Bev' played for the Probables, my former Bridgend team-mate Viv Jenkins and I for the Possibles. The Probables won but not before we'd given them a run for their money as the 38–29 scoreline indicated.

When Wales began the Five Nations, against England at the Arms Park, Gerald and John started where they had left off in the last match of 1972, against the All Blacks. John scored two of the five Welsh tries that day and Gerald one, facts which made them automatic choices.

All I could do was keep knocking on the door so that in the event of a change being forced by injury I would be ready to go in at a moment's notice. When 'Bev' was declared unfit for the home match against Ireland, I was sure my time had come at last.

Instead the Big Five selectors picked Jim Shanklin of London Welsh on the left wing, switching him from centre where he had played for the Probables in the final trial a few weeks' earlier. Despite Jim keeping his place for the last fixture of the championship, against France in Paris a fortnight later, I made the trip as one of two reserves, not back to Colombes but to the Parc des Princes which had been transformed from a run-down stadium into a 50,000-all-seater at a cost of £7million.

Cliff Jones, then chairman of the Big Five, made the announcement after Sunday training at the Afan Lido in Port Talbot. Substitutes were only permitted then in the event of injury and selectors would usually pick players with the versatility to cover more than one position, rather than specialists.

I was thrilled and surprised in equal measure to hear my name called out as one of four subs along with the Aberavon scrum half Clive Shell, the Cardiff back row forward Roger Lane and the Bridgend outside half Ian Lewis. The lovely coincidence about it was that we had all been in college together and there we were sitting on the bench waiting to be called on by Wales in the Five Nations.

Only one of us made it onto the field that day, 24 March 1973. I was the lucky one and doubly lucky in that Arthur Lewis, the Ebbw Vale centre, went out of his way to give me advance notice that he would be coming off and I'd be going on. Arthur, who was playing alongside Roy Bergiers, took me to a quiet corner of the dressing room just before kick-off and whispered in my ear: 'You may get capped this afternoon. Keep warm and make sure you're ready.'

I didn't think any more of it. Instead I took my seat at the back of the stand assuming that I was there just to make up the numbers. All that changed dramatically at half-time when Arthur came off and I went on. Gerry Lewis, the physio, was trying to massage my legs in what little time there was, because the half-time break then only lasted a couple of minutes at the very most. Jim Shanklin moved into the centre and I went on the left wing.

I was up and running straight away, going outside a few opponents on the wing and making quite an impression with my pace. Even though we lost 12–3, I'd made it at last and having waited so long to get the jersey I would be in no hurry to let it go. Luckily, I was a permanent fixture for the next 30 internationals, a run of ever-presence topped only by Gareth Edwards and Mervyn Davies of that era. Like them, I was never dropped. Talk about being in exclusive company!

Whenever Clive Rowlands joins us and the reminiscences begin, he will invariably touch upon one of his favourite themes: 'Don't forget boys, I dropped you all.' I'm not slow to put him straight: 'Clive, you didn't drop Gareth, you didn't drop Mervyn and you never dropped me.'

To this day, I am not sure whether Arthur came off because he was injured or because he felt I'd served my time on the fringes of the team. He didn't look particularly injured and I asked him later that evening whether he'd done it just to get me on. Arthur just laughed but, if he did, it was a wonderfully magnanimous gesture.

Nobody does the after-match banquet in more style than the French and that Parisian night in the splendour of one of the city's oldest and poshest hotels was memorable for all sorts of reasons. There I was in my dicky bow and penguin suit sitting with the superstars of world rugby, wishing that my parents had been alive to see it.

The presentation of caps at the after-match dinner is one of the game's oldest traditions. Naturally enough, I was looking forward to being presented with mine, all the more so because the French dinners were done in such style. This one, at the Hôtel Lutetia which had been the Paris headquarters of the Gestapo after the Nazi occupation of France some years before I entered the world, would be no exception. They had everything you could possibly want to eat and drink. What they didn't have was my cap and that wasn't their fault.

Instead of receiving it from the then president of the Welsh Rugby Union, Les Spence, I had to remain uncapped a little longer. The cap eventually arrived, through the post and I was no less thrilled for that. Another dream had been fulfilled.

Something else happened that weekend in Paris. It was the night when the confusion of having two players of the same name in the same team ended, when the two John Williamses were shortened to a set of initials.

It took the cockiness of a London Welsh flanker, John Taylor, to come up with a solution which has stood the test of time. Taylor approached me over a drink and said: 'Right. From now on you are JJ and you (pointing to the other John Williams) are JPR.'

We did not have to wait long for the opportunity to play together under our new, heavily abbreviated names. As part of their centenary celebrations, the Scottish Rugby Union staged an international seven-a-side tournament at Murrayfield on 7 April 1973.

As the home of sevens, Scotland put on a wonderful show and we were very keen to do it justice by sending our strongest possible team – Gerald, Gareth, Benny, Merve, John Taylor, the newly-christened JPR and the equally newly-christened JJ. As a back-up, we had the Neath prop Glyn Shaw and my mate from Bridgend, Ian Lewis or 'Mull' as we called him, and the Aberavon scrum half.

We got there and back in the finest amateur tradition, taking time off our various jobs and making it under our own steam. An international team making that same trip today from Cardiff to Edinburgh would have everything done for them but we were happy to meet a week before departure and make our own travel arrangements.

Gareth said: 'Let's go by car and leave on Thursday morning.' Gerry Lewis, the physio, drove one, Clive Rowlands, the coach, drove the other.

We decided to aim for Kendal and stay there overnight. Gareth the Gourmet knew of a 'fabulous' restaurant in the town so we went there, drove on to Edinburgh the next morning, and were staggered to find what appeared to be thousands of Welsh fans greeting us outside our hotel, the North British.

My first thought was how the hell could we get to the reception desk to check-in? The fans stepped aside and made way for us. I'd never seen anything like it, a parting of the Red Sea. We thought we had a real chance of rewarding the supporters by winning the tournament, which only goes to show how wrong you can be.

The event featured eight teams split into two pools of four with the winner of each meeting in the final. We were up against France, New Zealand and England. We swamped the All Blacks in the first game and did the same to France in the second which put us in a good frame of mind for the semi-final against the old enemy.

Their nine-man squad was an impressive one: Keith Fielding, David Duckham, Peter Rossborough, Peter Preece, Steve Smith, Roger Uttley, John Gray, Andy Ripley and their captain, Fran Cotton. A prop playing sevens? And not just any old prop but one of the biggest around.

Fielding and Ripley had already competed in the original series of *Superstars*, a television programme with which I would become familiar in years to come. In his book, Cotton told the England coach, John Elders: 'Christ, John, I'll need a motor-bike to keep up with that lot. But I was assured that my job wasn't to run tries in from sixty yards but to win the ball in both tight and loose whilst making my considerable presence felt when the opposition had the ball.'

He thought Wales made the mistake of putting too much emphasis on pace and too little on winning the ball. In hindsight, it was easy to see that one specialist forward, Taylor, was not enough. England had three – Cotton, Ripley and Gray – and it showed.

Murrayfield was packed to the rafters and we were confident that if we got any kind of decent ball we would get to the final. The only trouble was that we hardly got our hands on it. Cotton reckoned that England only allowed us to touch it three times.

I don't know about that but what I do know is that they were too smart for us on the day. We lost 24–10 and then had no option but to sit back and watch England beat Ireland in the final a little later that evening. Soon I would be doing something far more exciting – taking off on my first tour with Wales as a capped player in late May 1973.

And when we touched down in Toronto who should be waiting there, just as he said he would but Spence McTavish, the Canadian wing who talked me into letting him have my Wales jersey after the match in Cardiff at the start of the season. He looked like a Viking warrior so he tended to stand out even in the biggest crowd and, just to give me an extra special welcome, he was wearing my Wales jersey – or what was left of it.

To my horror, I could see that he had turned it into a sleeveless number. He'd cut both sleeves off and converted it into a drinking jersey. I never did get round to asking him what he had done with the sleeves. It was grand to see Spence again, although I had made a mental note that he wouldn't be taking the scissors to another of my jerseys at the end of this trip.

To be rubbing shoulders with the greats who had gone

on the '71 Lions tour – JPR, Gerald Davies, Arthur Lewis, John Bevan, Gareth Edwards, Delme Thomas, John Taylor and Mike Roberts – was a real privilege for a new boy like me.

I don't know if some people took the trip as seriously as they should have done and maybe a few treated it as their swansong. Put it this way, they certainly knew how to enjoy themselves, especially the London Welsh boys.

After landing in Toronto, we had a four-hour wait for our connecting flight to Vancouver and the opening match against British Columbia. True to form, the WRU had accepted an invitation to go to the Black Label brewery in downtown Toronto and have a few beers to while away the time.

Before we got off the plane, it would have been clear as crystal to members of the Toronto Welsh Society waiting to greet us that some players were a bit the worse for wear, and that's putting it politely. Mervyn led the way, wearing a straw hat, no shoes, and a fag in one hand, followed by his London Welsh pals in a similarly legless condition.

And that was before they got anywhere near the brewery so you can imagine what they were like when we got back onto the plane four hours later. Talk about drinking for Wales…

Once we checked into our hotel in Vancouver, Clive Rowlands as coach read the riot act, making it very clear in his own way that we were here to fly the flag for Wales and show the Canadians why we were one of the best teams in the world.

The Canadians had improved since I'd been out there with Bridgend the year before but they were still no match for Wales. While British Columbia proved a notable exception, some of the other fixtures were far too easy as the cricket scores illustrated and they would have been bigger still had the pitches not been so narrow.

To cater for the rising public interest we played in a few

stadia specially made for American Football which meant they were two metres shorter in breadth than international rugby grounds. It reduced the width and expansion of our game but I made the most of it to ensure that I would finish the tour as I'd finished the Five Nations in Paris three months before – on the wing for Wales.

Clive was so keen to pick me on one wing with John Bevan on the other that he moved Gerald into the centre which was where he played his early matches for Wales. I think Gerald quite liked the idea but it didn't work out and not only because of injury.

Midfield tactics were changing with the crash-ball centre as introduced by the All Blacks in the late 1960s when they used Graham Thorne as a battering ram the way Wales subsequently used Ray Gravell and, more recently, Jamie Roberts. Phil Bennett thrived on the concept because possession from second-phase ball enabled him to cause so much more havoc than he could from first-phase.

With Gerald ruled out by injury from the match against Canada on 9 June 1973, Clive's plan had been undermined. I felt confident about keeping my position whatever happened, even if the competition was out of the top drawer to say the least.

The issue resolved itself that September when John Bevan signed for Warrington at the start of a very successful career in rugby league which took him all the way into the Great Britain team. John was only 22 when he left and the mind boggles at what he might have achieved in Union had he stayed.

When he scored against Canada we had no idea that it would be his last try for Wales. We got nine all told, won 58–20 in baking heat and gave a crowd of around 12,000 – huge by Canadian standards – good value for their money. Caps would be given today but not then because the WRU didn't think it was worthy of Test-match status or maybe because it saved them a bit on the manufacture of caps.

For me it was a full-blown international, my first start for Wales and I remember it fondly for those reasons. And this, for the record, is how we lined up at the Varsity Stadium, Toronto:

JPR Williams (London Welsh), JJ Williams (Llanelli), Keith Hughes (London Welsh), Arthur Lewis (Ebbw Vale), John Bevan (Cardiff); Phil Bennett (Llanelli), Gareth Edwards (Cardiff, capt); Glyn Shaw (Neath), Jeff Young (London Welsh), Phil Llewellyn (Swansea); Mike Roberts (London Welsh), Delme Thomas (Llanelli); Tommy David (Llanelli), Mervyn Davies (Swansea), John Taylor (London Welsh).

CHAPTER 5

Unbeatable

Peter Jackson

FOR MOST OF the second half of the 20th century, an ugly blotch marred the sporting landscape of the world. The apartheid system that divided South Africa into a society segregated on strictly racial lines turned the country into a pariah.

Apartheid, an Afrikaans word for the concept of being apart, had been made law in 1948 by the all-white government of the National Party headed by DF Malan. It would take the rest of the world time to show its abhorrence at the racist regime and by the mid-1970s, South Africa had been expelled from the two biggest events in global sport.

In 1961 they were kicked out of football's self-proclaimed universal brotherhood, FIFA. Some three years later, in August 1964, the International Olympic Committee came to the same conclusion in respect of South Africa a few weeks before the opening of the 18th summer games.

Before the end of the decade, New Zealand rugby and English cricket had also washed their hands of the racist regime. The South African government's refusal to accept any non-white member of the All Blacks, an unfortunate title in the circumstances, led to the cancellation of their 1967 tour of the Republic.

The following year, in September 1968, the MCC did likewise in respect of their scheduled visit that winter in protest at South African objection to the England party including Basil D'Olivieira, a Cape Coloured from Cape Town who had qualified for England after joining Worcestershire.

In the spring of 1974, Harold Wilson's newly-elected Government stopped short of outlawing the Lions trip to South Africa that summer. Instead, he urged the rugby authorities to call it off, a request which, not surprisingly, fell on deaf ears.

Rugby, seen by many back then as the most reactionary of sports, stuck stubbornly to its policy of maintaining contact.

There had been disruption from mass demonstrations by the anti-apartheid movement as orchestrated by the young Peter Hain. He even organised a sit-in protest at the Lions' team hotel and held a private meeting with the tour captain, the Ulsterman Willie John McBride.

In his congratulatory circular letter to the chosen few, tour manager Alun Thomas made it crystal clear that certain information had to be treated as classified. Where the Lions would be staying pre-departure and when they would be flying out were 'highly confidential' matters with the word confidential underlined.

Thomas' letter also acknowledged the political storm swirling around the tour. 'Anyone unduly troubled by Mr Peter Hain or has "a conscience about coming", do ring me first before doing anything. Reverse the charge if you must.'

It can be safely assumed that nobody felt sufficiently bothered to take up his offer, even though some would have been sorely tempted to take advantage of the unusual generosity of a Union executive offering to pay for the call.

Like Mrs Thatcher, the Lions were not for turning. And so they took off for Johannesburg, the first British (and Irish) team to be disowned by the British Government. Wilson's Labour Government wanted nothing to do with the Lions.

They instructed British Embassy staff to shun the crème de la crème of British rugby. In her role as Under Secretary of State for Foreign and Commonwealth Affairs, the late Joan Lestor told Embassy officials to withdraw all hospitality and receptions for the team and officials.

Ted Heath, back in opposition as leader of the Conservative party after they had lost the general election within three months of the tour's scheduled start, wasted no time urging the Lions to ignore the Government and proceed as planned.

By then, one player had removed himself from consideration for the tour because of his anti-apartheid stand based on what he saw of South Africa on the previous Lions' visit there in 1968. John Taylor, of London Welsh and Wales, admitted that he realised only when he got there that he had made a mistake.

'I put all the misgivings to the back of my mind, believed all the twaddle about building bridges and that we were not supporting apartheid and as soon as I got there I realised very much that we were,' he said during an interview with Simon Turnbull in *The Independent*. 'The really big decision was not to make myself available for the Wales-Springboks game over here in 1969–70.

'In '74 the Lions were going through the motions with the invitation letter because they knew what the answer was before they even sent it out. But '74 was the big deal. I was absolutely convinced that the rest of the sporting world was right and that there was still this sort of massive arrogance in rugby, that the brotherhood of rugby, the fraternity of rugby meant more than the brotherhood of man and that they couldn't be bad chaps because they played rugby. It was very much that sort of arrogance that I absolutely deplored in rugby.'

Willie John McBride, the captain, never had any doubts. 'The debate over apartheid was raging,' he wrote in his autobiography of pre-tour hostility. 'One school of thought was that connections should be kept open through tours, so that the South Africans could be gently persuaded to the viewpoint of the outside world as to the horrors and impracticalities of the apartheid system.

'The contrary view was that all ties should be cut, thereby isolating South Africa from the outside world. I strongly favoured the first option but a lot of people were against the tour. When the Four Home Unions' Tours Committee reiterated their determination to see the tour through, [Harold] Wilson instructed all the embassies in South Africa to sever any ties with the touring party.

'Now I'm a member of the British Empire and that was not a very pleasant message to my ears. In fact, it deeply annoyed me but I never discussed it at the time.

'Once the touring squad had been announced, there was a lot of pressure on the individual players. They were being telephoned by outsiders and urged not to go. I didn't want the tour to fall down but I knew that if it was going to, it would do so before we left.'

The conflicting views of Taylor and McBride are worth recalling as an example of the emotive maelstrom engulfing the tour before it took place. While the IOC and FIFA had signified their revulsion of apartheid by suspending South Africa, the International Rugby Board stood resolutely by one of its founding members, even after the four home unions had aborted the Lions tour of South Africa scheduled for 1985.

The same sheer bloody-mindedness that ensured that the Lions of 1974 would not succumb to political pressure proved invaluable once they got down to business on the pitch. The Lions didn't just beat every team that the South Africans threw at them but, when push came to shove, they beat them up for good measure.

This would be no ordinary tour but one like no other for reasons that had nothing to do with politics.

Invincibility is a rare quality in individual sport, rarer still when applied to international teams on tour overseas. Rocky Marciano retired as the undefeated heavyweight champion of the world but even Mark Spitz, the only Olympian to win seven gold medals at one Games, knew what it was like to be beaten into second place.

In rugby union, Cliff Porter's 1924–5 All Blacks had set an impossibly high standard. They played 32 matches in Britain, Ireland, France and Canada, starting in September 1924, finishing in February 1925. They won every single match by an average score of 26–3.

In cricket, Sir Donald Bradman's 1948 Australians achieved their own invincibility over a similar five-month period. Unbeaten and unbeatable, they won 25 matches and drew the other nine, almost all of which they would have won had it not been for rain and the periodic rearguard action.

Along the way they broke all manner of records, not least that for the most runs in one day – 721 in six hours against Essex at Southend, an average of 120 an hour. Bradman (who else?) led the charge with 187 in a shade more than two hours.

Extraordinary teams produce extraordinary results. When the Lions took off into the blue yonder from Heathrow airport in that first week of May 1974, not even those in charge of the mission could have imagined how extraordinary they would prove to be in some of the most hostile places on the rugby planet.

Astonishingly, given their punishing schedule and the unforgiving state of grounds baked hard by the tropical sun, they were able to complete the four-match Test series without making anything other than two changes – Andy Irvine for an injured Billy Steele on the left wing, Chris Ralston for the equally injured Gordon Brown in the last Test.

As McBride said, by way of tribute to the endurance of his fellow Lions: 'The players have medics these days. We had Elastoplast...'

They also had a wing who could do more than run like the wind, a comparative lightweight at no more than 12 stone who would rise above the recurring re-enactment of the Anglo Boer war and fulfill the role of the Lions' executioner-in-chief.

JJ

THE POLITICAL FALLOUT probably affected me more than most for two reasons: I was a schoolteacher employed by Mid Glamorgan Education Authority and all the education authorities in south Wales were Labour controlled. They didn't beat about the bush when it came to stating their position on granting me leave of absence from my position as PE teacher at Maesteg Comprehensive School.

'You can go,' they said. 'But we won't be paying you.'

I knew what that meant – four months without wages which would effectively stretch to six months because I wouldn't be reporting back for duty until the beginning of the school term in the September. Although Jane was also teaching, it left me with a nagging question: How am I going to pay the mortgage?

I ought to make it clear right from the start that I would not have sacrificed my place on that Lions tour no matter how great the personal cost. With our combined salaries, we could just about manage, so it was a massive sacrifice but one I was prepared to make without question.

I had to be a British Lion. Maybe I could not afford to go on the tour but what was equally true was that I could not afford *not* to go. The way I saw it, this was the equivalent of competing at the Olympics. Because of the cost involved, I *had* to do well. I had no excuse not to.

We had bought a property in Maesteg and it had to be paid for but we would manage. I kept telling myself that without ever believing that we would. Believe me, teachers were not particularly well paid then, not that I am suggesting they are now.

And then, out of the blue, I was invited to meet a coloured South African gentleman, Mr Van Zyl, at his home near Bridgend. He owned a few cinemas in the area and he asked me to drop in for a cup of tea and a chat about South Africa, the place and its people.

Like many of my team-mates, I didn't have a clue what the word apartheid meant. Mr Van Zyl enlightened me as to the history of South Africa and I owed him a debt of gratitude that he had gone to such lengths on my behalf. I was not to know then that the debt of gratitude I owed him would probably be far greater than I could imagine.

I phoned Jane on a regular basis during the tour, anxious to find out how she was and just as anxious to find out about the mortgage. Jane told me not to worry, that everything was under control which was her lovely way of ensuring that no domestic matter got in the way of my ambition to win a Test place and then keep it.

One of the first things I did after returning home from the tour four months later was to see my bank manager, Mr Evans, in Maesteg. I wanted to explain to him a matter uppermost in my mind and to ask for his patience and understanding.

'I'm sorry Mr Evans but due to being away with the Lions on unpaid leave, I haven't been able to meet the mortgage repayments,' I said.

'Oh, but you have,' he replied.

I was so overcome with relief that I didn't say much more.

Where did the money come from? I have always suspected that dear old Mr Van Zyl paid it out of his own pocket although I shall never know for sure.

It was all part of the most amazing sequence of events of my rugby life, a period of almost unending success, from Llanelli beating the All Blacks to my first cap for Wales, from Llanelli thrashing Cardiff in the Welsh Cup final at the Arms Park to a record home win over the Wallabies and my first international try – all topped off by the Lions tour of South Africa.

The trip first crossed my mind as a serious opportunity on a summer's day in August 1973 during Llanelli's pre-season tour of Canada. Carwyn James arranged it as a reward to the team for earning enough silverware to justify an extension to the trophy cabinet at Stradey Park.

We went coast-to-coast, from Montreal in the east across thousands of miles to Vancouver in the west. And it was there, during a barbecue on Vancouver Island, that Tommy David mentioned the Lions. Tommy had only come out for the last leg of the Canada tour and from what he told me, I realised that he was pacing himself for a season which would run over the best part of the next 11 months.

'I've been told there's a good chance of me going on the Lions tour,' he said. 'So I want to make sure that I pace myself and don't play too much.'

Nobody from the inner sanctum had said anything to me about the Lions tour. Neither had Phil Bennett nor Roy Bergiers had any indication about the trip that all three of us would be making at the end of the 1973–4 season. How Tommy got the nod so early I still do not know. I can only presume he had bumped into the Lions coach, Syd Millar, and that Syd had told him: 'Tommy, I want you on that tour with me.'

In typically cocky Pontypridd fashion, Tommy must have

thought: That's it, then. I'm on the tour. Better make sure I'm fit and ready for it.

The only problem was that somebody else was first-choice for Wales at the time and that somebody else was none other than Dai Morris. There was no question that Tommy was an outstanding back row forward, one of the best I ever played with. He had an immense ability as a ball-carrier, a quality which stood him in good stead when he went to rugby league.

Tommy's a very close friend of mine and maybe that's why I've always said of him: 'Tommy David is the only person I know who is even uglier than his Grog!'

Then I'm off sharpish, as if I'm back in my blocks and under starter's orders.

What he said that evening on Vancouver Island got me thinking. Hmmm, wouldn't it be something to be a British Lion? John Bevan had gone north. I felt I would be an automatic choice for Wales – me on one wing, Gerald Davies on the other. And that was how it turned out for every international that season, starting with a 24–0 win over an unusually nondescript Australian team.

Some of the central figures in the 1971 Grand Slam, like Barry John, Delme Thomas, Jeff Young, had retired, Barry ridiculously so at the age of 27 when he could easily have made another Lions tour to follow his magical performances against the All Blacks during the victorious series in 1971.

A new-look side had a special reason for wanting to win the Five Nations in addition to all the thousands of usual ones. This would be Clive Rowlands' last season as national coach and we wanted to see him off in the style he deserved.

We beat Scotland first up at the Arms Park 6–0 thanks to an early try from Terry Cobner on his debut. The second match, Ireland in Dublin on a very blustery winter's afternoon, ended all-square at 9–9 but at least I had the satisfaction of scoring my first try for my country.

Gareth Edwards put me away on the blindside of a scrum for a simple run-in from about 15 metres, about as straightforward as you could get. 'Well done,' said Gareth and when I shrugged my shoulders as if to say it wasn't any big deal, he took me to task. 'Don't play it down. I've seen many players miss simple tries. Always remember, they're worth four points whether you run 'em in from behind your own posts or from a foot.'

France in Cardiff at full-strength would be a more severe test of our title ambitions. Again we had to settle for a draw, 16-all this time, and again I scored a try and, in complete contrast to the one at Lansdowne Road a fortnight earlier, this was something else – my best-ever for Wales.

We won the ball from a line-out and it went swiftly across the back line to me on the left wing. Instead of flying onto the ball at pace, I had to stop and take it standing still. My intention was to go outside the opposing wing, Roland Bertranne, and as he cut inside to make the tackle, I grubber kicked the ball behind him. It sat up perfectly for me, I kneed it on over the try-line and ran past at least two French defenders and touched it down in the corner.

It was, by anyone's standard, a great try made out of nothing. A wing's job is to score tries but the very best of them are capable of producing that bit of magic, especially when the team needs a lift. People were starting to recognise me as someone who had that ability.

Rugby World magazine called me 'The Welsh Wonder Wing' which was very flattering. To be put in the same bracket as Gerald gave me a terrific boost. Moving into the highest category made me confident that I would be picked by the Lions because I was one of the best in the four home countries.

David Duckham had decided he would not make himself available for Lions selection before we ran into each other during the last match of the championship, England at Twickenham. This one was extra special. A win would make us champions instead of Ireland and give Clive the best possible send-off.

We had the backs to polish England off despite losing JPR to injury just when everyone began to believe in him as an indestructible presence. Our concern wasn't at full back, where Roger Blyth came in for his first cap, but elsewhere.

Throughout that campaign we had struggled to impose forward domination. England had a whole battery of world-class forwards – Fran Cotton, John Pullin, Mike Burton, Chris Ralston, Roger Uttley and Tony Neary. We didn't lose any sleep over them because we knew that if we got some ball, we'd beat them.

It was still anyone's match midway through the second half when we won a line-out and set about mauling our way downfield. All of a sudden, the ball popped out of nowhere straight into my hands. A gap opened up, almost as if somebody up there was looking after me, and, whoosh, I went clean through it.

As I approached the England full back, Dusty Hare, I did my usual trick and chipped the ball beyond his reach. As it bounced towards the left corner of the in-goal area, Duckham came across from the opposite wing and Peter Squires, the other wing, turned to give chase.

The three of us went flat out for the line in front of the North Stand. I got there first and fell on the ball. From that day to this I never needed to look at the videotape for confirmation because as I landed on the ball, the point of it struck me in the stomach. I was winded but my elation at scoring eased the pain and I jumped up in the air.

'Yes,' I said to myself. 'We're going to win this game and

we'll be out in London town tonight as champions of the Five Nations.'

Imagine then my horror when I saw the referee, John West of Ireland, who must have been almost 20 metres away, disallow the try and blow for a 22 drop-out to England. The Welsh fans began booing. I stood there aghast. Duckham and Squires were still within earshot and I turned round and said to them: 'That was a try.' And they agreed with me. Yes, it was but once they'd got back into the dressing room, they decided that no, it wasn't a try.

The touch judge on that left-hand side happened to be a RFU committee man. If only technology had arrived 30 years sooner, we could have begged Mr West to signal to the TMO and ask him: Try, yes or no?

Another refereeing mistake cost us dearly that day as well. Phil Bennett broke clean through a few minutes later and England were in dire trouble until the referee decided not to play advantage and brought us back instead for our feed into a scrum. Believe you me, such decisions drive you mad.

England won 16–12 and Ireland were champions. We were robbed of the title that day and Jack Young, the chairman of the Big Five selection committee, used the very same words in the dressing room. We were livid.

For a while John West became Public Enemy No. 1 in Wales. To be fair to him, he did send me a Christmas card for the next ten years or so but I never quite found it in me to reciprocate.

Max Boyce's song about 'Blind Irish Referees' ensured that the incident has gone down in folklore, not that Mr West has ever admitted to making a mistake. More than 30 years later, he was still sticking to his guns that he made the right decision.

At the after-match dinner in the West End, the English players, like 'Burto', Neary and Squires, gave me some stick but

I didn't mind that so much. It wasn't their fault and, besides, they were all top guys, and still are. I was livid but at least the imminent selection of the Lions squad for South Africa gave me something else to think about that weekend.

The rugby writers of the national dailies and Sundays published their squads and I found my name in nearly all of them. I was expecting to be picked but you never know until someone from the Lions either rings you up and tells you or the letter drops through your front door.

Tom Grace from Ireland, Billy Steele of Scotland and another Welshman, Clive Rees, were the other wings. Gerald's name was conspicuous by its absence but only because he had chosen not to make himself available. He had been on the last Lions trip to South Africa six years earlier and I have since read that he had serious concerns about revisiting the country because of apartheid.

To be picked as a Lion, which meant you were one of the best players in the four home countries, was a big thrill. I had been considered good enough to perform at the very highest level of my sport. I may not have made the Olympics as a sprinter but I would be going off to the rugby equivalent.

First, though, there was a very important domestic matter to be attended to, the Welsh Cup final against Aberavon at the Arms Park. These were great showpiece occasions played before huge crowds and, as the holders, retaining the Cup meant a lot to the players and the supporters.

Three other Llanelli players were also going on the Lions tour, Phil Bennett, Roy Bergiers and Tommy David. Phil decided he was not going to run the risk of getting injured and pulled out of the final. Therefore, Roy, Tommy and I felt obliged to go with Phil's decision and we also pulled out.

We still won the Cup but what we did was wrong. It was a selfish decision and if I had my time over again I would have played in that final against Aberavon. Top sportsmen have to be selfish at times during their careers but I let the club down and the supporters down that day. We all went to Cardiff with the team to give them our moral support. We should have played. The club should have come first in view of everything they had done for us.

Before we knew it, we were assembling in London as British and Irish Lions. There can never have been an assembly like the one we experienced with all sorts of anti-apartheid demonstrations going on outside the hotel and we players just trying to keep our heads down and our spirits up.

The tour had been used as a political football for weeks and when I arrived at our hotel in London the place was besieged. It was typical of McBride to confront the problem at the very start. We met in a conference room and he made this powerful speech which had a galvanising effect on everyone who heard it.

He said he appreciated the pressures we had been put under, not that I, for one, felt any such pressures. He said there would be doubts in some of our minds, not that I had any doubts. And then he said it again: 'If you have any doubts about going on this tour, stand up and say so now. Anyone with doubts about this tour will be of no use to me and no use to the team. So if that's how you feel, be man enough to say so and leave the room.'

Behind us the doors had been left open. Nobody, of course, was going to go but Willie John had to address the issue and he did so to maximum effect. We left that room and set forth on the adventure with an unbreakable will to succeed and an unshakeable faith in our ability to deliver the goods.

I only had one thought on my mind, to make sure I played rugby worthy of my new status as a British Lion. In political terms, we were naïve, unaware of the country's racist laws. We were going there to win a Test series for Britain and Ireland

and if by doing so we improved the lot of the downtrodden, all well and good.

Would I have gone had I known what I knew by the end of the tour? Yes, I would. By going we experienced the apartheid system at first hand. And many times during the tour, black South Africans would come to us and say: 'Thank you for coming. Thank you for showing the world that the white supremacists who treat us like second- and third-class citizens are not so supreme after all.'

We had highlighted South Africa's internal issue to the world's press.

I always thought the Welsh were crazy about rugby but the South Africans were crazier by far. When we landed at Jan Smuts airport in Johannesburg, there must have been about 2,500 people waiting to welcome us. We knew right away that we had flown into a cauldron and, thankfully, there would be no escape from it wherever we went.

Luckily, we had people who had been there before – Gareth Edwards, the coach Syd Millar, and Wille John himself. They knew what was coming once we had gone through the process of acclimatising which was another crazy experience in itself.

We drove for what seemed like a hundred miles out onto the High Veldt, across vast tracks of countryside which looked like the Brecon Beacons except that it was about 50 times bigger and the grass was yellow instead of green. We stayed at Stilfontein, an old gold-mining town some 6,000 feet above sea level in the north-west of the country.

Ken Kennedy, the Irish hooker who doubled up as a doctor, issued us with these salt tablets which I was skeptical about because of my background in athletics. It all seemed very basic but there was no question that Dr Kennedy had got it spot-on.

We knew how to train to the maximum effect and how

to get the most out of those lung-bursting runs at altitude. We knew how to look after ourselves. We were supremely conditioned from start to finish.

The Lions then were very different to the Lions now, especially in terms of a back-up team. We had 30 players, a manager (Alun Thomas) and a coach (Millar). We acquired the services of a physio once we got to South Africa although he wasn't much more than a rub-a-dub man.

Compare that with the size of the management entourage when the Lions were in South Africa in 2009 and Australia four years later. They had specialist coaches for everything. We had none of that. When I injured a knee in one of the very early matches, I sorted it out myself. That was really how it was.

All that helped make the whole squad tough mentally as well as physically. You were on your own to an extent. It was up to you what you made of the tour. The competition for Test places was fierce, so fierce that you kept playing with the odd injury because you couldn't afford to give anyone else a chance.

We had to be tough to survive in that environment. The amazing part of that tour was that in spite of the constant struggle to keep half a step ahead of your rival, we were all the best of pals. Many of us made friendships then which have stood the test of time since and will go on doing so for as long as we live.

Millar and McBride were ahead of their time. They had a plan based on their determination to ensure that this time the Lions would not be pushed around the way they had been on previous tours of South Africa. As befitting men who were strong in mind and body, these Lions were not going to be intimidated. There would be no backward steps when the mucky stuff hit the fan.

The philosophy was strikingly simple: it didn't matter how

we won, as long as we won. We did so on a scale which nobody could have envisaged, averaging five tries per match over 22 matches. We scored nine in our first match, against Western Transvaal at Potchefstroom and the margin of the victory, 59–13, would have left the Springboks in no doubt what they would be up against.

For a sprinter, I was unusually slow getting out of the blocks. I didn't play in the first match, drew blanks in the second and third, then sat out the fourth. The next fixture took us to a seaside town on the Garden Route between Cape Town and Durban.

I'd never heard of Mossel Bay until I got there aboard a small Dakota aircraft but I've remembered it ever since. At last I was up and running in a way that I could never have dreamt of. The opposition, South-Western Districts, were such a mismatch for the Lions that we scored 16 tries and I got six of them – a double hat-trick.

I could have had eight and would have done had JPR not dummied the last defender when we had a two-on-one. He only had to draw the last man and pass for me to have strolled over but each time he went over himself. Still six was a decent haul, even if there was a price to be paid.

Towards the end my opposing wing, who had every reason to have been sick of the sight of me, hit me with a late tackle which knocked me into another world. I spent the night confined to bed, in no fit state to join the celebrations and unaware at that stage that we had missed the chance to give a future England cricketer the runaround.

Allan Lamb, later to become a famous England batsman, told me after the match that he hoped to make the South-Western Districts team in the centre but they'd dropped him. Fancy being dropped from a team that was walloped 97–0, or 113–0 because the try has since been upgraded to five points? Had Allan played, nobody would have doubted his courage – a quality he displayed by the bucketful in scoring centuries against the fearsome battery of West Indian fast bowlers in the 1980s.

We scored at Mossel Bay from the first minute to the last. In one afternoon, I'd gone from being nowhere on the Lions try chart to top scorer and that made me confident of getting into the team for the first Test coming up in ten days' time.

Selection for the last midweek fixture before the big one is often a sign that you've missed out and I'd been picked on the Tuesday of Test week against the Proteas, a team of coloured players built around Errol Tobias who went on to become a Springbok.

The pack that day included five forwards who I considered Test certainties – Fran Cotton, Gordon Brown, Fergus Slattery, Roger Uttley and Mervyn Davies. I found it very reassuring to be among such company while I was aware that of the three other wings, Clive Rees and Billy Steele were going well. The other, Tom Grace of Ireland, had been hit by an untimely injury.

After the bonanza in Mossel Bay, I had to settle for one try against the Proteas, a historic fixture because they were the first black team to play the Lions. After the match, played in front of 20,000 people at the Goodwood Stadium in a suburb of Cape Town, we were showered with gifts by local kids in the township where they held a reception for us.

Errol Tobias made a name for himself that day as a fine attacking fly half and some seven years later he deservedly became a Springbok Test player. We scored five more tries against the Proteas, continuing to ensure we never missed an opportunity to send a warning out to the whole of South African rugby that this was a Lions team like no other.

They never seemed to take the hint until it was too late. After every home defeat, they'd say: 'Wait till you get to P.E. (Port Elizabeth). They'll sort you out.'

And then after we'd won in P.E., they'd say: 'Wait till you get to Cape Town. Western Province will sort you out.'

After we'd beaten them and the Springboks at the same venue in the first Test, they'd say: 'Wait till you get to Jo'burg. Transvaal will sort you out.' And when we'd beaten them they said: 'Wait till you get to the Free State. They'll sort you out.'

And they very nearly did, going closer to beating us than anyone else. In the end, nobody ever sorted us out but we sure sorted them out, starting with the opening Test at Newlands in Cape Town. For as long as I live I shall treasure the moment I walked into the dressing room and saw my Lions jersey hanging on the peg.

I thought of all the famous players who had worn it down the years. I thought how as a boy growing up in Nantyffyllon I'd first heard about the British Lions and never even dared to dream that one day I would be good enough to play for them. And the last thing I did before pulling the jersey on was to look around at Willie John McBride and all the other great Lions in that dressing room. And I was one of them!

And then the horrible reality struck me in the opening minutes like a slap in the face that if I continued the way I'd started, maybe I wouldn't be one of them for much longer. It had been tipping down with rain for hours and the consequent mudbath meant it was never going to be a day for the backs to run the ball.

We were only about 15 minutes into the match when one of the Springboks kicked the ball into space behind me on the left touchline. JPR came across and collected it. We had a set-play for such an eventuality which we practiced in training. It involved me running round behind JPR to offer him the option of passing.

He gave me a pass all right but, for some reason, he did it while I was facing my own in-goal area with my back to the opposition. From such a dangerous position, I tried to run across the field, away from the Springboks bearing down on me. I aimed a hopeful kick to touch. Instead the ball sliced off my foot and ended up touch in-goal.

With one of my first touches of the ball, I'd given away a five-yard scrum. The mess that I'd put my team in was about to get a whole lot worse when Dawie Snyman, the 'Boks outside half, dropped a goal to give South Africa the lead. I thought to myself: You stupid so-and-so.

I knew I had to redeem myself while not letting the blunder get to me. Our forward dominance was so pronounced that there was never any doubt about the result. Three Bennett penalties and a drop goal from Edwards saw us home comfortably at 12–3 and my early blunder had been forgotten.

The win had a devastating effect on the very foundations of South African rugby. It was so devastating that before the second Test in Pretoria a fortnight later, the Springboks locked themselves up in the city's maximum-security jail. They must have been the first international team to be sent to prison for losing a Test match.

They had been heavily criticised in the papers and on the radio and must have been grateful that the country had no television. Taking them out of the normal hotel environment and putting them in the clink was one way of keeping the players out of the public eye but it seemed an extreme reaction.

When we heard about it, we wondered: 'Why have they done that?' We sensed that they were in a state of panic and that encouraged us to go for the kill, to make it two-nil with two to play. What we achieved that afternoon on the burnt grass of Lotus Versfeld will rank forever as one of the most brilliant victories by any Lions team anywhere.

The 'Boks altered virtually half their team, including both half backs. They also made changes on the wing, in the centre, two in the front row and at No. 8. We put out the same team and answered all the jibes about the Lions being a ten-man team by running them off their feet in the grand manner.

I knew I had to do something to compensate for my error in the first match. My chance came early on and I wasn't going to let it slip. Gareth Edwards kicked down the blindside, I beat the full back to the ball and toed it on over the line for the first try.

Shortly after that I got another, finishing off a wonderful move started by Phil Bennett on his own line. When he set off with his dancing feet, I followed him instinctively as I always did when we were playing together for Llanelli knowing that, more often than not, Phil would cause havoc.

Some great inter-passing between Mervyn Davies, Gordon Brown and Willie John, opened up the 'Boks. Edwards and Roger Uttley kept it going and I was there to finish it off. Two tries in the first half of what ended up as the biggest Lions win over the Springboks of all time. After the cock-up in Cape Town, I had redressed the balance.

Nobody had scored two tries in a Lions Test before, not that I was going to settle for that. I was looking for a hat-trick and I think I'd have got it later in the match if only Fergus Slattery had passed the ball. Sometimes you needed a crowbar to get the ball off him and that was certainly one occasion when it would have come in handy!

Our domination that day was so complete that had the match gone on for another ten minutes, I swear we would have scored 50 points. Still 28–9 represented a historic win. At the end the contrast of emotions between the teams had to be seen to be believed – wild jubilation on one side, utter despair on the other.

They were still miserable when we went to a hotel in Pretoria for the after-match function but nothing was going to put a damper on our celebrations. As luck would have it,

I happened to be on a table with Mervyn Davies and some of the other big lads who liked a drink.

Every place on the table had been set, complete with a large, long-stemmed wine glass. Merve then took over. He cut the stem off every glass which he then filled to the brim with white wine which more or less had to be knocked back in one because there was no way you could put your glass back on the table because of the jagged end where the stem had been.

Within half an hour we were roaring drunk. From memory, Merve carried on right through until the next morning when we were heading off for a few days of R and R in the Kruger National Park.

So there he is at Jan Smuts airport on the Sunday morning, in his straw hat, shirt-tail flapping, flip-flops, and a fag in his hand. Despite a night on the tiles, Merve is hard at work, loading crate after crate of beer onto the plane. This, believe it or not, was the man who had destroyed the Springbok back row, the man who had stopped the great Jan Ellis in his tracks with one of the greatest tackles I have ever seen. That morning at Jan Smuts, the star of the Lions pack looked like Robinson Crusoe.

That was Merve – work hard, play hard. He would party like nobody else and, believe me, he had some competition, nobody more so than JPR. If you drank six cans of beer, he'd drink seven. If you stayed up until one o'clock in the morning, he'd stay up until two.

Just as he would not be beaten on the field, so he wouldn't be beaten off, it except that Merve was something else. And then he would turn up for training and perform as though he'd had an early night with nothing stronger than a cup of cocoa. Like everyone else, the only thing that mattered to him was for the Lions to stay invincible.

Every time we won, on a Wednesday and a Saturday, we'd climb onto the bus and someone like Mike Burton, the England prop, would shout out: 'Six gone and we're still unbeaten.' Then it was seven gone, still unbeaten until at the end we were able to say: 'Twenty-two gone, still unbeaten and nobody left to beat.'

The Springboks were used to bullying whoever they came up against at the holy temples of South African rugby, places like Newlands, Loftus Versfeld, Boet Erasmus and Ellis Park. They were never going to bully the Lions because when they tried, we gave it back to them in spades.

When I say 'we', I mean the hard men because people like Phil Bennett, Ian McGeechan and a few others, including myself, were out of it. McBride laid down the law, that whenever any of us were victims of foul play, the rest of the team would get stuck in, big time – 'You belt the guy nearest to you as hard as you can.'

That philosophy of 'one in, all in' led to the birth of the '99' call which has passed into Lions folklore. Willie John says he came up with '999' as the emergency call but then reduced it by one digit when others thought it was too long. Bobby Windsor, never a man to mince his words, said in his book, *The Iron Duke*, that he thought it was 'a load of bollocks'.

My hearing may have been slightly defective or maybe I was just standing too far away out on the wing but I must confess I never heard the 99 call. JPR insists he did and that there definitely was such a call. If it was used as the cue for an all-in fight, then it must have been used on a regular basis because there was an awful lot of fighting on the field and some of it was ferocious.

There were very few television cameras covering the games and the TMO wouldn't be invented for at least another 30 years. If there had been red cards then, the referees throughout South Africa would probably have kept them in their pockets because hardly anyone ever got sent off. You could get away with blue murder and some of my team-mates did.

When a mass brawl broke out, the poor old referee in the middle of the mayhem had no chance. It was on such a scale that he could have sent four, five or six off at any given time but, of course, he was never going to do any such thing. Winning the fights, as well as the rugby, sent a powerful message to the Springboks – these Lions are tough. They brought a hard-edged attitude which the South Africans had not encountered during previous Lions' tours.

The fisticuffs did lead to some hilarious incidents, like the one during what was unquestionably our toughest match, against the Orange Free State in Bloemfontein before a vast crowd of nearly 60,000. The Free State had gone out of their way to make us welcome, as every city and town did but Bloemfontein really did it with style and imagination.

For example, when we landed, a fleet of open-top vintage cars were waiting for us and we rode into the city in a cavalcade. The word was out, these Lions were special and the Free State had put on a lavish welcome. They also thought they were better than the South Africa national team, that they could beat us up and do what the 'Boks had failed to do in the first two Tests.

The stadium in Bloemfontein was packed, the grass was yellow, the pitch rock hard with a cinder track around it, and the sun was hot. The Free Staters were out to strike a blow for the damaged reputation of the white man's sport in South Africa and boy did they strike some blows! They came raining in from all directions so it was just as well that we were prepared for what was to come and that our 'one in, all in' defence system was in proper working order.

They had a one-eyed second row forward, Johan de Bruyn, who looked as fearsome as his reputation. Everything out on the yellow grass that day seemed to be stacked against us, including the referee, a South African, because nobody then had thought of the idea of appointing neutral ones.

Mike Burton, who could slug it out with the best, tells the story of how McBride approached him at half-time with a plan of action to reduce de Bruyn's influence as the leader of the powerful Free State pack. According to 'Burto', McBride said to him: 'Mickey, you're going to have to stoop to the lowest of the low and hit him in his good eye.'

Whatever happened, it must have been some punch because it dislodged de Bruyn's glass eye. It must have been the only time that a Lions' match was stopped while both teams combed the grass for a glass eye. Eventually someone found it and de Bruyn stuck it back in.

The late Gordon Brown who was marking him in the line-out, took one look at him and said: 'My God. There's a bit of grass sticking out from a corner of his eye.'

Staying in one piece was hard enough without all the fighting. The brutality could not disguise the fact that we were struggling and one of the main reasons why was over the loss of both our fly-halves. Phil was injured and the other No. 10, Alan Old of England, had gone home after breaking a leg. Ian McGeechan filled the gap but the loss of Bennett and Old meant we didn't have a recognised goal-kicker.

De Bruyn and his Free Staters very nearly had the last laugh because we were losing 9–7 going into injury time. This had all the intensity of a proper Test match. They matched us in the set-scrums and while we were always confident we could pull something out of the bag, this was getting desperately close for comfort.

That desperation was reflected in an incident near the end when Willie John went careering into one of the Free State tight forwards from a line-out five metres from the home try-line and knocked him senseless. The medics came on, the player was staggering all over the place, and that was when our skipper got really smart.

'He's got to go off,' McBride told the referee, knowing that there probably wouldn't be time for the Free State to get a substitute on for what was the last scrum of the match. And that is exactly what happened with disastrous consequences for the home team. They packed down a man short and we took full advantage. Our pack rolled them back, Mervyn Davies picked up at the base and gave it to Gareth Edwards.

He went down the blindside and had a go himself for the line and got half-collared. He didn't see me so I shouted 'inside'. With that he threw the ball over his shoulder and I caught it coming in off the left wing, saw the gap and scored the winner. It was probably the best example of that telepathy which Gareth and I shared, an ability to know instinctively that in the heat of the moment we were on the same wavelength.

Of all the tries I scored maybe that was the most important one of all because it saved our unbeaten record.

When the final whistle went, I sprinted for the dressing room like a bat out of hell. Crowds poured onto the field at the end of every match on that tour and there was always the risk that some Afrikaner with a grudge would clobber you one. That happened to Willie John at the end of the second Test and he had a go back. Imagine that happening today. It would be headline news, sent round the world in a flash.

Going into the after-match reception, we were a mightily relieved bunch. The reception was held in a church hall, an unlikely setting considering some of the brutality which had taken place in the stadium. The Free State captain looked like a man who had been in a war zone, with his head swathed in bandages and the blood seeping through.

When he got up to speak, the blood was dripping down his nose and then falling onto the microphone which he was holding in his hand. Every so often, you could hear the amplified sound of the blood on the mic, like the clip-clop of a horse's hooves.

We did our best to keep straight faces but the Free State

skipper's pay-off line was even more hilarious than the sound of his blood – 'I want to thank the Lions for a good, clean, hard game...'

If that was a good, clean, hard game, I'd hate to have seen his version of a dirty, nasty one! By then we had won the first two Tests and reduced the 'Boks to a state of almost blind panic. We had out-scrummaged them from start to finish at Newlands and thrashed them five to nil on tries at Loftus Versfeld. They couldn't understand what had hit them. Orange Free State at Bloemfontein had been almost their last roll of the dice.

They kept making wholesale changes and we kept winning. They made 11 for the decisive third Test at the Boet Erasmus Stadium in Port Elizabeth and we beat them by virtually the same margin as we had in the second Test, only this time it was 26–9 instead of 28–9.

And there was another striking similarity. I scored two tries on each occasion, something which had never been done before in Lions' Test matches and which has never been done in the 40-odd years since. The 'Boks didn't know where to turn next. The word was that on the morning of the third Test they still hadn't decided who would play scrum half so you can imagine our surprise when they ran out with their No. 8, Gerrie Sonnekus, wearing No. 9.

He might have been playing in the scrum half position but he didn't have the skills for the job. Even so, the 'Boks hit us with the biggest onslaught we had experienced, one which left us fighting for our lives. One hallmark of a good team is the ability to absorb the pressure, hold firm and then hit them just before half-time which was exactly what we did.

Gordon Brown scored a try minutes before half-time, cashing in on a line-out error by the 'Boks. That meant they had 40 minutes in which to save the series and their pride. The second half had just started when the punch-up of all punch-ups broke out. The 'Boks were fighting for their rugby lives.

'Broonie' found himself in the thick of the almighty brawl. I am not exaggerating when I say that he hit the deck four times. He went up and down like a yo-yo. Each time one punch forced him down, 'Broonie' got straight back up.

There must have been 16 players all throwing punches. One of theirs went off with a broken hand which he'd smashed against somebody's head. And when the fight blew itself out, do you know what the referee did? He could have sent several players off but he didn't even bother giving anyone a warning. Instead he blew for a line-out – Lions' ball!

It's a miracle that Gordon could stand on his own two feet unaided. Willie John McBride didn't waste any time giving his Scottish colleague any sympathy. Instead he called for Bobby Windsor to throw to Gordon who leapt like a salmon and palmed it into Gareth Edwards' hands.

His long spin pass found Phil Bennett. The ball went rapidly down the line, from Benny to Ian McGeechan, to Dick Milliken. At that point JPR hit the line from full back on a dummy run. Dick fired a long pass to me on the wing, a move that we had rehearsed again and again on the training ground.

As I sprinted for the corner, the cover defence came across. I passed the ball back inside to JPR who gave it straight back and I ran diagonally to the posts, moving fast enough to avoid being tripped up by an attempted ankle-tap from the Springbok skipper, Hannes Marais.

Of all the tries I scored, this was one of the very best because of the perfection of its creation. It had the devastating effect on South Africa of knocking the stuffing out of them. Although I was given due praise, it was a perfect team try that we had practiced a thousand times in training.

A few minutes later the ball was hoofed upfield. JPR

gathered and threw a long pass to Milliken who passed to me around halfway. I chipped the ball over the defensive line, caught it on the bounce and dived in at the corner, my best individual try.

Again what made that so satisfying was that it showed we could pull out the stops when it mattered most. Skill at the vital moment shines through under pressure only if it comes as second nature. That only comes from hours and hours of practice until it becomes perfect because you know the day will come when you will have to do it for real.

That day duly came at Boet Erasmus in Port Elizabeth. For all we had gone through in the previous 12 weeks, all the scrummaging, the mauling and the fighting, we showed South Africa we had the high-speed skills to win a four-match Test series undefeated and score tries to match the best scored any time, anywhere.

I shall always treasure the reaction to that second try. As I jogged back to my position for the re-start, the whole crowd stood to applaud the Lions. It was as if they were saying: 'You have taught us a massive lesson on how rugby should be played.' That was the most satisfying moment of the entire tour.

You can defend against most things but not pace. Clive Rowlands always said that you make your own luck in rugby and in that respect nobody summed it up better than a South African, the golfer Gary Player. When he chipped in off the green and a spectator dismissed it as lucky, Mr Player said to him: 'You know, it's a funny thing. The harder I practice, the luckier I get…'

It was tough on Marais. He'd done wonderfully well to get close enough to make the attempt to tackle me but the loss of the series meant that he shouldered most of the blame. Once we had recovered from the battering, we proceeded to produce what I regard as the finest 40 minutes of my life on a rugby field, not that that would have been any consolation for Marais.

One of my most treasured photographs is one of me sprinting round behind the Springbok posts to touch the ball down, not because it's me but because of the reaction of the black people in the crowd. The sheer joy on their faces, the arms raised in a victory salute at another Lions try is something I still marvel at after all these years.

Their jubilation stemmed from the sight of the all-white South African team being hammered by the Lions. They were effectively saying to us: 'Thank you for showing that this white supremacist regime running our country is not so supreme after all. Thank you for coming. Thank you for beating them.'

The Springboks had been treated as rugby gods in South Africa, a team that could do no wrong. Against us in 1974 they could do no right and part of the reason was that they had been isolated from other international arenas because the world disapproved of apartheid.

What we didn't appreciate at the time was that those who had been thrown in jail for objecting to apartheid were also rooting for us. I was told that Steve Tshwete, who became Minister of Sport after the first free elections, listened to our matches on the radio and cheered every time we scored. I was supposed to have been one of Nelson Mandela's favourite players and you can't ask for a bigger compliment.

Going into that final Test with the series in the bag, we were still highly motivated if, understandably, a little tired. Our bags were packed for home and so we had to keep reminding ourselves that the job, like the Springboks, still had to be finished off and that somehow we had to make sure we didn't fall at the last fence.

We were not as dominant up front in that last match at Ellis Park as we had been and one reason for that was that the

Springboks were considerably better at the end of the series than they had been at the start. In the end we had to settle for a draw which at least meant we had completed the 22-match tour without losing but, in truth, we ought to have made it a 22nd straight win.

JPR made a break late on, Fergus Slattery looped round him and I would certainly have scored in the corner had 'Slatts' given me the ball. Instead he went for the line himself and got the ball down but, surprise, surprise, the South African referee, Max Baise, disallowed it.

Bobby Windsor, the indestructible hooker from Pontypool, has since said that when he protested to Mr Baise, the referee said to him: 'Look boys, you're going home. I've got to live here...'

We couldn't really complain because earlier in the series Roger Uttley was credited with scoring a try which was dubious to say the least in that one of the Springboks probably touched it down first.

At the final whistle, I made a bolt for the dressing room. When the crowd invade the pitch, as they always did on that tour, you never know what's going to happen to you which is why I was never going to hang around to find out. Some of the bigger lads carried Willie John off and there was absolute bedlam in the dressing room.

The supporters joined us in the celebrations which was great because they had made the long trek to cheer us on at considerable personal cost. My brother Ken was among them, so was Stan Thomas or Sir Stanley as he is now and he provided us with no shortage of champagne.

We felt on top of the world which I suppose we were. It was a wonderful feeling and while people talked about the '99' call and the fighting, there was no escaping the fact that we'd scored some of the best tries the Lions have ever scored.

What we had accomplished would take some time to sink

in. We only had a very sketchy idea of how the tour had been followed back in the UK and the massive welcome at Heathrow on our return made us realise that we had all done something truly historic.

It's amazing to turn the clock back to that first conversation about the Lions during Llanelli's Canadian tour and to think what we had achieved over a period of 11 months. It's even more amazing to know that more than 40 years later, the '74 Lions are feted whenever we get together and wherever we go. The great sadness is that recent reunions have had to take place without three of the very best – Mervyn Davies, Andy Ripley and Gordon Brown, all three unique characters from a tour unique in British sport.

For every one of us, life would never be the same again. Thousands turned up at Heathrow airport to cheer us home, including a bus load from Nantyffyllon RFC. The Minister for Sport, Dennis Howell, was there, his public relations machine working overtime. He welcomed us with open arms and acclaimed our series victory as something to be applauded by everyone – all very different to the message from the same Government a few months earlier.

Once I had been reunited with Jane, it was then off on the final leg of the journey home to Maesteg. I didn't have a clue that as soon as we arrived, Paul Hughes, the Nantyffyllon chairman, would be there having arranged to take us to the village in a horse-drawn carriage.

That wasn't the only amazing part of the day. As the horse took Jane and I gently along a journey of some three miles, people lined every inch of the route. It was as if everybody in the locality had turned out and, to cap it all, Max Boyce was there to sing us home as only he can.

It was a welcome fit for a king and a queen. What my own people did for me that day is something I will never forget even if I live to be a hundred. I shall forever be in their debt.

CHAPTER 6

Banned and banned again!

Peter Jackson

MONEY HAD BEEN a dirty word in rugby union for a long time before those fine, upright custodians of the amateur game had George Parsons thrown off the train taking their team to Paris for a Five Nations match towards the end of the frozen winter of 1947.

Even by rugby standards, it still beggars belief that a player chosen to represent his country one day could be arbitrarily declared *persona non grata* the next. A policeman from Pontypool, Parsons had committed no crime in going about his daily duty of enforcing law and order but the WRU suspected that he had been offered a sum of money from a rugby league club.

That, they decided, was sufficient reason to assume guilt and ensure that their second row forward was left stranded on the platform of Newport station as the steam engine belched towards the Severn Tunnel and on its smokey way to Paddington.

Just as blacks in the southern states of America were not allowed to sit with whites on public transport under the segregation laws in force until the mid-1960s, so anyone who had had any contact with those dreadful professional clubs in northern England could not sit with bona fide amateurs, presumably for fear of contaminating them.

Parsons, a genial man who clearly subscribed to the view that life was too short to hold any permanent grudges, had to wait almost 30 years before the WRU plucked up the courage to do the decent thing and present him with the cap which he had won against England at Cardiff Arms Park in January 1947.

'It's good to know that after so long there is no malice,' he told me some years before his death in 2009 at the age of 83. 'The Union were wrong when I was put off the train that day. At the time I didn't have the slightest intention of going North even though some 20 rugby league clubs had been in touch with me. It wasn't until the following season that I began to listen to them.'

He signed for St Helens in 1948 and went on to play almost 300 times for the club, including their losing Challenge Cup final against Huddersfield at Wembley in 1953. Among those whom he was forced to leave without a word of farewell in the compartment at Newport station that day was the prince of centres, Bleddyn Williams.

Years later he made no attempt to disguise his disgust at Parsons' treatment by the autocratic Captain Walter Rees, a WRU secretary who sounded as though he had graduated from the Joseph Stalin school of administration. The merest suspicion tended to result in condemnation.

'On that basis the entire Welsh team had probably been professionalised,' Williams said. 'Everyone had been approached at some stage or other. What they did to George was an absolute disgrace.'

According to the archaic rules relating to amateurism, any Union player who talked to anyone from rugby league was immediately found guilty as charged, even if he had no intention of committing the heinous crime of 'going North', a geographical euphemism for selling your soul for a suitcase full of the old white five pound notes.

Cliff Morgan, then a 22-year-old student, found himself confronted by that very scenario when a deputation from Wigan came knocking on the front door of his parents' home in Trebanog in the Rhondda Valley. Those on the receiving end could do nothing, of course, to prevent men bearing gifts from the north of England descending upon them out of the blue, but in the unforgiving cold war between the codes that was enough for a lifetime ban. Cliff must have avoided such a fate on the grounds that word of the approach never got out.

White fivers had been spread over the kitchen tables of homes across England from the early days of the RFU. In their desire to keep the game as one to be played strictly for fun, they had been holding inquiries into allegations of payment long before the Great Schism of 1895 resulted in 22 northern clubs breaking away over the Union's refusal to allow their players broken-time payment as compensation for missing work on Saturday mornings.

JJ

ON THE SUNDAY before we played England at the Arms Park in February 1975, five of the Wales team chosen the previous week were called into a private room at our usual training base in the Afan Lido sports centre on Aberavon beach. All five were told they could not take to the field against England as selected because all five had been accused of taking money for a match.

This story has never been told, until now. I know it to be true because I was one of the five and of all the ludicrous examples of alleged breaches of the amateur regulations this was the most ludicrous one of all. Imagine the uproar had the story got out at the time – Wales ban five in cash scandal.

And what a five they were – Gareth Edwards, Phil Bennett, Mervyn Davies, Bobby Windsor and myself. None of us could believe what we were hearing when the chairman of selectors, Keith Rowlands, called us into a small room before we went out training and told us: 'Gentlemen, I have some bad news. None of you can play against England on Saturday.'

One of the spin-offs of the Lions' success was that we were in demand from the moment we got back home. The invitations to go here and play there came so thick and fast that you could have been out every night of the week. We took care to ration our acceptances.

Two weeks before the England match the five of us agreed to turn out for Newport Saracens in a charity fixture against the touring Canadians. We did so as a favour to the Saracens' most distinguished old boy, Bobby Windsor.

We played the match, got changed and went to the clubhouse for a bite to eat. There was a massive reception and the club treasurer slipped a £50 note into our pockets as a thankyou for coming and making sure we didn't lose out on expenses.

Nothing more was said until we reported for Wales training at the Afan Lido the following Sunday. That was when Keith Rowlands told us we could not play against England because we had been paid for playing in that game for Newport Saracens.

We looked at each other aghast, aghast not just as the thought of not playing against England but aghast in equal measure that we had been accused of taking money for playing. Clive Rowlands, who'd become one of the Big Five after retiring the previous season as national coach, was also there. We could tell from the body language of Clive and Keith that neither was comfortable with what they had to say. They were very much on our side but they were also under strict orders from the Union hierarchy. There could be no soft-pedalling on this one.

We asked what we had done wrong and it then transpired that a member of the Welsh Rugby Union, a district representative, had seen us being slipped this money and had reported it to the Union. They, in turn, had been obliged to look into it.

The Messrs Rowlands told us very clearly that unless we paid the money back, and paid it back right away, we could not play against England. We gave back our £50's but if I had known then what I knew a few years later, I'd have said to the Welsh Rugby Union: 'Go on, play without us and see what happens. You'll be made to look a bloody laughing stock.'

Can you imagine the furore it would have created? Can you imagine how silly the WRU would have looked and, by extension, the entire game of rugby union? We handed the money back and were told to submit an expenses claim instead. And guess what the expenses claim amounted to? Fifty pounds per person.

That somebody felt it necessary to snitch on us raised a question which nagged me all the way through my time with Wales. Why did the committee men go out of their way to cause trouble for us? What made them jealous? How come that they rode on the back of our success but when it came to us making a fiver here or there they went out of their way to embarrass and trouble us?

They had so many perks as a direct result of our success on the field, swanning around in the best of hotels with their wives on weekends in London, Paris, Edinburgh and Dublin, all at the Union's expense. But if we wanted to take our wives, we had to pay for them.

When it came to the players getting a perk, there always seemed to be some member of the committee going behind our backs and reporting us. Don't forget, we were world stars in those days. Television was becoming a big player in the game with their readiness to start paying big bucks and that was all because of what we were doing on the field – free, gratis and for nothing.

We all played against England, as selected, the following Saturday as though nothing had happened. We were told to keep quiet about it and concentrate on beating England which we did, as usual in those days, this time by a margin of 20–4.

The pettiness of the officials never ceased to amaze me. The worst example happened a few hours before we lost to England at Twickenham the previous year and this really did make my blood boil, not only because it was so pathetically trivial but that I was confronted about it at a time when I was concentrating on what I had to do that afternoon.

We had a team meeting in a private room at the Kensington Palace Hotel at 10.30 in the morning. I'd never played for Wales at Twickenham before and the whole focus was on getting the win that would give us the Five Nations title which we wanted for ourselves, of course, but most of all, for Clive Rowlands before he rode off into the sunset.

Shortly after midday we were in the dining room of the hotel grabbing a last bite to eat. Some of the forwards tucked into steaks and Bobby Windsor would order the biggest one they had in the kitchen. He'd eat half of it and wrap the other half up in a serviette, stick it in his bag and get stuck into it after the match.

He liked his pound of meat did Bob, although several pounds might have been nearer the mark.

I made do with honey and toast. So we were on one side of the dining room and the committee and their wives were on the other. I'm thinking about what kind of reception England have planned for us at Twickenham when there's a tap on my shoulder.

I look up and Jack Young, the chairman of the Big Five, is standing behind me. 'JJ,' he says. 'Bill Clement (WRU secretary) has been checking your expenses. You've claimed £5.'

So I tell him: 'That's correct, Jack. Two trips from Maesteg to Cardiff and back, so I put down a round figure. Petrol isn't cheap these days, you know.'

Then Jack says: 'We worked it out at £3.80. You owe us £1.20.'

I can hardly believe what I'm hearing. So there I am, in the dining room just about to play for Wales at Twickenham, and I'm having to dig into my pocket and give the chairman of the Big Five a pound note and a 20 pence coin. The fans had paid top dollar to be there that afternoon, England-Wales always generated colossal amounts of money from crowds of nearly 70,000 and there I was having to stump up because the Union decided I had over-charged them.

We were the ones producing the goods, making the game more and more attractive so that the Unions could get fatter and fatter contracts from television. You would have thought they would have been only too pleased to help us instead of nit-picking. It was as if they took delight in pulling us down a peg or two. Or was it a case of the top officials not keeping pace with a rapidly-changing game?

Jane never felt comfortable going to away matches with the committee wives. She often used to say: 'I feel like an intruder at a private party.' Jane should have been made welcome as the belle of the ball, not treated like an outsider who had no right to be there.

Perhaps it was just as well that Jack Young caught me when he did. Had he left it until Monday, which he ought to have done, I'd like to think I would have told him to f*** off and shove the expenses claim where the sun doesn't shine.

I was still only in my first full season with Wales so it was probably best that I'd paid the money back without making a scene. The only person in that Wales team who was never afraid to tell the committee what he thought of them and to ask them the questions we wanted answered was JPR. As the undisputed king of the full backs and therefore undroppable, he was vociferous in his criticism of the committee.

A pity that a few more of the senior players didn't speak up in support of JPR. He probably paid a price for telling the committee what he thought of them and that price cost him the presidency of the Union when he stood against Glanmor Griffiths and lost. Even now, after all these years, I believe they are still wary of JPR.

The more successful we became as players, for Wales and the Lions, the more the Union seemed to delight in bringing us to heel. Six months after the petty business over my £5 expenses claim, the Union tried to have me drummed out of the game as a professional.

The row revolved around an offer I'd had to sign for Widnes Rugby League Club. My contribution to the Lions tour had not gone unnoticed and suddenly I was made aware of how much I was worth on the open market.

Vince Karalius, one of the greats of rugby league, came to my house in Maesteg very early one Monday morning just before Jane and I set off to work as teachers at our respective schools. Mr Karalius arrived in the biggest Mercedes the town of Maesteg had ever seen.

We explained that we had to be in school by nine o'clock that morning so we didn't really have time for a chat. With that, Vince went straight to the point of why he had driven from the north-west of England all the way to south Wales. He reached inside his pocket and wrote out a cheque for £13,500.

Thirteen thousand, five hundred pounds! The new house Jane and I were living in had only cost us £4,500. So here was a famous rugby league man representing a famous rugby league club willing to pay me the equivalent of three houses to sign a piece of paper.

Because I didn't want to be late for school, I said: 'No, no, Mr Karalius. I can't sign that. I've got to get to school.'

When we got back from school that afternoon, he was still waiting. Since our first chat in the morning, he had upped the offer by another £3,000 to £16,500. We were talking now of a world-record fee for a player from Union. At the very least, I had to consider it. I'd have been a fool not to.

And I'd hardly begun to consider it when the phone rang. Peter Jackson of the *Daily Mail* said he'd heard about the offer and wanted to check with me to establish that it was true. I told him it was and I told him that I was considering it. When Peter asked me if he could quote me on that, I told him to go ahead. He warned me that I could fall foul of the amateur regulations. I said: 'What are they going to do? Ban me? Go ahead and quote me.'

The next day, I did an interview with BBC Wales television saying that I had thought about the offer and that I had turned it down. I was staying with Llanelli because playing for the Scarlets and Wales mattered more to me than all the gold in the north of England.

I thought nothing more of it. I drove down to Llanelli on the Saturday morning for their game that day against Swansea. I wanted to arrange some tickets for my brothers to collect that day and went to see the Llanelli secretary, Ken Jones. He said to me: 'Sorry JJ, you can't play this afternoon.'

I said: 'Ken, what the hell do you mean?'

He said: 'Bill Clement's been on the phone. He said you have professionalised yourself.'

'Ken what do you mean, I've professionalised myself?'

'He said that you considered an offer from rugby league and that's enough to get you banned for life.'

'Ken, for goodness sake. If someone made you an offer

which was worth more than four times the value of the house you were living in, wouldn't you stop and consider it? Come on, wouldn't you?'

Dear Ken was a good friend, one of those selfless volunteers who were the backbone of Welsh rugby. He knew it was all nonsense but the Union bigwigs in Cardiff had told him that I had professionalised myself and that I could not play that afternoon. So he had no choice but to carry out the instruction. What a farce!

I said: 'Ken, if this gets out there will be one hell of a scandal. Anyway, if I'm banned, you and everyone else might end up banned as well for talking to me.'

I was livid. I jumped into my car and drove straight home, not knowing what to think because it was all too silly for words. The more I thought about it, the more incensed I became.

I thought of all the sacrifices I'd made just for the honour of playing the game. I'd gone six months without pay to go on the Lions tour. I'd been short-changed by the jealous small-minded men on the Union committee and now I'd just been told that I'd been kicked out of the game! For what? For being honest enough to say I had considered a world-record offer from a rugby league club.

I considered it and turned it down – no thankyou, Mr Karalius, I'm staying with Llanelli. The WRU saw fit to make me feel that I had committed some sort of crime when all I had done was decline a fortune for the glory of continuing to play for Wales for nothing. They should have been rushing to shake my hand instead of shaking me by the throat.

Between Saturday afternoon and the following Monday somebody somewhere saw the situation for what it was, a monstrous overreaction. I don't know whether Ken had a quiet word in the right ear but something happened because nobody ever raised the subject with me again.

I drove to Stradey for training as usual that Monday evening not knowing whether the Union had hired a few bouncers to bar me from training. I was made as welcome as I'd ever been and it was as if my banishment from the match the previous Saturday had never happened.

My hunch was that the WRU knew they were in the wrong and that the best way to get themselves out of the mess was to let the matter drop. They knew they had no right to do what they did but it is still a source of anger that they treated me with such total disrespect.

Maybe they didn't like the way the game was changing, that individual members of the Wales team were becoming far bigger than the men running the Union. A lot of water would flow under a lot of bridges before Will Carling got himself into trouble for calling the RFU's flabby general committee '57 old farts'. In the mid-1970s, we called our Union worse names than that except that none of them ended up in print.

The jealousy persisted. Many years later, a committee man came up to Gareth Edwards and asked him: 'Are you a millionaire?' That was the sort of attitude we were up against.

So they threatened to ban me twice in one season – in September 1974 and less than six months later in February 1975. They would have banned me again not long afterwards had they known about a payment which I kept to myself.

We felt that we were being taken for a ride. There was a growing feeling amongst the squad that if we were asked to play extra games for fundraising purposes, then the people organising those games should slip us a little something.

We'd look at the vast crowds for international matches and ask ourselves: 'Where's all the money going?' We were beginning to ask more and more questions. It was a time when some wonderfully generous employers were giving international players jobs on the company payroll with as much time off as they needed.

I was never given a cheque for playing a game of rugby. Nor would I ever have asked for one. Had I wanted that, I would have signed for Widnes. Llanelli were always very fair in that they spared no expense to put us up in the best hotels and book us into the best restaurants because Carwyn James wouldn't have it any other way.

No matter how many television interviews any of us did, we were never allowed to keep the money. The WRU made sure we donated it either to a charity or to our local rugby club.

Other new opportunities were beginning to emerge as people recognised the growing fame of rugby players. New programmes like *Superstars* came along featuring an all-star cast who would compete in a variety of disciplines from different sports. It had a big following and very soon there was some serious money to be won.

I was competing against professional footballers like Joe Jordan and Terry Yorath. They were allowed to keep their money but I had to give mine to my national rugby union as did all the other international rugby players. I got £500 and a portable television set for taking part in *Superstars* at Grangemouth. They paid the £500 directly to the WRU but at least they allowed me to keep the television set, presumably on the basis that it wasn't worth very much.

Sometimes you got the impression from Bill Clement that he ran a detective agency as well as the WRU. At times it felt a bit like a master and servant relationship, with the Union doing all the mastery and the players doing all the serving.

One day Mr Clement rang Phil Bennett and said to him: 'I've got the £50 cheque you got for taking part in the *Superstars* programme. I see that you've been on again but you haven't send us the £50 cheque for that one.'

At that point Phil had to explain to him that the programme

was a repeat and that there was no repeat fee. You wondered why they were so petty but they kept on doing it and the worst example of penny-pinching happened on the journey back to Wales after we'd beaten England at Twickenham in February 1976.

No rooms were made available at the hotel for our wives. So on the Saturday night of the England match Ray Gravell and his then wife, Eirona, and my wife Jane and I all stayed in the same room. Over breakfast on the Sunday morning, we asked whether our wives could have a lift back on the coach to Cardiff and the Union gave us their permission.

We stopped for lunch at Swindon and, naturally enough, our wives had a bite to eat as well. We thought nothing more of it until three days later when a letter from the WRU came through the post and you'll never believe what was inside – a bill for Jane's Sunday lunch.

This was a very strange way of the Union showing its gratitude to us for turning up at Twickenham, beating England in front of some 75,000 people and millions more on television and taking the first victorious step to what would be a Grand Slam. And this was how they thanked us. Why were they so mean when they were so rich? Why couldn't they have just paid the wives' lunch themselves? No wonder we felt they were taking advantage of us at every turn. No wonder our attitudes began to harden.

We were again the victims of their stinginess at the end of that championship. In honour of our Grand Slam victory, the Prime Minister, James Callaghan, MP for Cardiff South-East, invited the team and their wives or girlfriends to a reception at No. 10 Downing Street.

As amateur players who had given up precious time from work and home throughout that season, the WRU could have made it a real treat for us. They could have given us first-class travel by rail to Paddington in recognition of a first-class job.

They could have put us up in London overnight and made it a real occasion.

Instead we went by bus and came straight back on the bus after the reception. We all needed somewhere to freshen up before going to No. 10 and suggested that the WRU booked us into a hotel. They turned that request down flat and made alternative arrangements for us to use the toilets at Scotland Yard.

Jane and the rest of the wives deserved something better than that but Rod Morgan, a senior police officer in the South Wales Constabulary and member of the WRU's general committee, knew somebody high up in the Metropolitan Police and that's how the arrangement came about.

And, most important of all, we could spend a penny without the Union spending a penny of theirs on us. Our success had put hundreds of thousand of pounds into the Union coffers and still they did everything on the cheap as far as the players were concerned – almost as if they had been paying us a fortune in wages! And yet, no matter how badly the WRU treated us, we couldn't wait to play for them. Looking back, we should never have stood for it.

The PM was very nice and seemed really pleased to meet us, as he ought to have been because it was good public relations for him and his Cardiff constituency.

In that respect, he probably got as much out of it as we did. I'd had enough with the Union's meanness and decided to get a bit of my own back without them being any the wiser.

Not long after the UK *Superstars*, I competed in the South African leg of the same event and was paid a substantial amount – £2,500, which was all the more substantial in the early 1980s. I was not allowed to keep a penny of it but I decided to keep the whole lot which meant I had to go through a farcical procedure.

First of all I gave the money to my solicitor. Then I gave it to the treasurer of Llanelli RFC on the understanding that he would give it back to me in due course. By then I'd started my industrial painting business and so that the club would not be seen breaking the rules of amateurism, they came up with a proposal.

'Look, John,' they said. 'Just to make sure it's all legal and above board can you paint the stand and then submit an invoice for the work?'

OK, so far so good. Then they said: 'John, can you just give the crush-barriers a lick of paint while you're at it?'

Eventually, I got my £2,500 back but not before I'd spent more than that painting the ground! Not one of my smarter pieces of business, that's for sure, but it was all good experience. Some were more rewarding than others and none more lucrative than the deal a lot of us did to wear a certain brand of boot.

The German company Adidas had made a big name for themselves in soccer and athletics before they began getting interested in rugby in the late 1960s. The word was that Horst Dassler, the son of the founding-father, was watching a France-Wales match and asked why Gareth Edwards, Barry John and other Welsh players were not wearing his boots.

Almost all the players at that time were using beautifully hand-stitched footwear made by GT Law & Son, a company based at Wimbledon Park, who were well-known in athletics and for good reason. When Roger Bannister broke the four-minute mile barrier at Iffley Road in Oxford in 1954, he was wearing spikes made by GT Law.

Times in rugby were changing. Once Herr Dassler let it be known that we ought to be wearing his boots, the players were not slow to see the opportunity of making a few bob without the green-eyed members of the WRU committee knowing anything about it.

At first they started painting the Adidas logo, the three

white stripes, onto our previously unmarked black boots. Soon it got more organised and we'd do our own private deals with Adidas, always assuming that their rep liked you and thought you were sufficiently high-profile to give the company free advertising.

They wanted the star names, the goal-kickers and the try-scorers. Luckily, I fitted the bill and got approached right away. We were paid on a match basis but nothing that was going to change my way of life.

Then you think of what 80 minutes exposure on terrestrial television was worth for Adidas in terms of advertising their product to six million or so armchair viewers. Mike Burton, who knew a thing or two about commercialism, said once that he reckoned a ten-second prime advertising slot on ITV then would set you back the best part of 30 grand.

'Burto' once told a story about one of his England team-mates in the 1970s who'd done deals with two companies to wear their products. Not being able to grow an extra pair of legs, he got round the problem by wearing one of each and probably doubled his money.

How the Unions didn't find out about it was beyond us, not that anyone was complaining. It was good while it lasted and it lasted a good few years before the *News of the World* spilt the beans and that was the end of it although, luckily, by then my international career had run its course.

The Unions then did what they should have done in the first place which was to organise their own boot deal and so ensure that the manufacturer paid them instead of the players. The boot scandal was big news and the RFU was forced into conducting an investigation into who was paid and how much.

Adidas admitted that they had paid about 50 'amateur' players but denied that anyone had got more than a four-figure sum. Mervyn Davies admitted that he'd got £50 a match and Glyn Shaw, the Neath prop, was so overjoyed with his £50 that he called Arthur Young, the Adidas rep, 'Santa Claus'.

Anyone found guilty would have banned for life. To his credit, Dassler never named any names and although the row rumbled on for a few months, the RFU closed the case without taking any action. The WRU did the same but anyone with half a brain could see where the game was heading.

Llanelli had an Adidas kit deal before Wales did a similar deal and I found myself at the centre of another bit of pure farce before a match against France. I found the white Adidas shorts that I wore for the Scarlets suited my running style better than the white Wales shorts so I brought them with me for the international.

Ray Williams, who was then secretary of the Welsh Rugby Union, came into the dressing room to wish us well. He looked me up and down, spotted the Adidas shorts and said: 'You can't wear those.'

I tried to explain to him that I ran better in them than the official Wales ones. I don't know whether Ray thought that by that I meant they were better for running in all the way to the bank. Anyway, I refused to change them and the compromise was to put a piece of sticking plaster over the offending logo. It can't have been that sticky because it fell off as we ran down the tunnel.

Nothing more was ever said but with players being asked to give up more and more of their free time to meet increasing demands as amateurs, the tide of professionalism had begun to roll. The concept of rugby union as a recreational game for gentlemen, as devised by the Victorian gentlemen of England, was on borrowed time.

CHAPTER 7

Carwyn

Peter Jackson

PETER REES REACHED the grand old age of 90 in February 2015, the last man standing from the first post-Second World War Five Nations Championship in 1947. He also deserves a special mention in the history of the game as a visionary who did British rugby the almighty favour of giving Carwyn James the first major platform for his creative talent.

As president of Llanelli RFC, Rees heard on the grapevine about James leaving Llandovery College and offered him a coaching position at Stradey Park. Few are better qualified on the subject of James the coach and nobody described him as perceptively as the former president: 'A player's man and a treasurer's nightmare. He had no trouble with the committee but the committee had trouble with him.'

If the England footballer Martin Peters really was ten years ahead of his time, as the World Cup-winning manager Sir Alf Ramsey said he was, then James could be said, without fear of contradiction, to have been at least 20 years ahead of his time, not least from first-hand experience of how other teams in other sports went about their business.

He went to Wigan to learn about their rugby league team and, most of all, he went to Old Trafford to learn about Manchester United, not as a welcome outsider but as a friend of the club's then manager, the late Dave Sexton. That was where James learnt the value of looking after the players, giving them the star treatment on the basis that they would be more likely to respond with star performances on a Saturday afternoon.

For all his success, still without precedent as far as the Lions in New Zealand are concerned, James became something of a prophet without honour in his own land. His failure to win election to the Welsh Rugby Union in 1969 as a district representative was nothing compared to the biggest single paradox of his life – that nobody ever gave him the chance to coach Wales.

Typically, he wanted it on his terms or not at all. Those terms revolved around the abolition of the Big Five selection committee. If the buck stopped with the coach in rugby, as it most certainly did just like the manager in football, then the coach had the right to pick the team he wanted as opposed to the one picked for him by the four others on the Big Five.

The famous James letter to the WRU, coinciding with the end of Clive Rowlands' six-year reign as coach, turned out to be both an application for the vacancy and a withdrawal on the basis that his conditions would never find acceptance.

In it, he writes:

I personally feel that changes are now necessary. These are my main points:
1. That the national team coach, as in some other countries, should always be the Chairman of Selectors.
2. That the Chairman of Selectors be allowed to choose two, three or even four advisers to help him – preferably three.
3. That preferably these would be coaches now active with their clubs.
4. That they would be chosen for their experience as players (forwards/backs) as coaches, and with reference to geography.
5. That the national team coach and his advisers should seek the assistance of all club coaches in Wales and attend club coaching sessions as from September. Wales, from a rugby point of view, is sufficiently small to put these ideas into practice. Elsewhere, they would be impracticable.

Wales has been at the forefront in its thinking in recent years. It is no use for WRU members to bemoan the fact that other countries are catching up with us. The answer surely is that we must always try and out-think them.

Having considered my position over and over again, I have reluctantly come to the conclusion that I mustn't allow my name to go forward. I know that I'm asking too much of the Union – that change takes time. But I felt, however, that it was only fair to make my views known for the sake of the appointment – we all want the new man to be successful. He must be given the freedom to express himself.

A coach, like a teacher, is an expression of personality and he has to dominate if he is to succeed. This he can't possibly do with a small committee who were responsible for his appointment. Whatever the future policy, it is important, as a matter of principle, that he is appointed by the full executive committee of the Union and he should always be answerable to them. The dictator must observe humility!

My questions were rhetorical and I don't expect a reply.

Yours faithfully,

Carwyn James

JJ

CARWYN'S MAGICAL REIGN over Llanelli ended at the close of the 1973–4 season. Clive Rowlands stood down as Wales coach at the same time so it was only natural that Carwyn would bow to popular opinion and put his name forward for the honour of being able to do for his country what he had done for the Lions and Llanelli. Most of all, that meant beating the All Blacks, something Wales hadn't done then for some 20 years and something they still haven't done in the 40 or so since.

Typically, Carwyn wanted to do the job his way. His views on exactly how were always going to be controversial. Most controversially of all, he wanted to do away with the Big Five, the selection committee whose name had become synonymous with the national team through good times and bad.

As his famous letter to the WRU shows, Carwyn had his

own definite ideas. As the coach who would stand or fall by his results, he made it clear that he would not accept the way things had always been done with the Big Five picking the team, with some consultation with the coach, then telling him to get on with the job of winning international matches.

He was fortunate to have had outstanding players at his disposal during the 1971 Lions series in New Zealand and he had been similarly fortunate during his time at Llanelli. It was typical of the man that he would do the job his way or not at all.

People say it was a crying shame that such a gifted, intelligent man never got to coach Wales. He was simply unique. What made him so was his eloquence and intellect on top of his massive knowledge and feel for the game. He could swear without ever losing his self-control. In the blood and thunder of the dressing room, he always kept cool and he looked cool, too, what with his double-breasted suit, hair slicked back and a cigarette, always a fag, between his fingers.

Intellectually, as well as in every other aspect, he towered above the committee. When he left, Llanelli were never the same again and I say that with the utmost respect for those who followed him, a tough job made all the tougher by Carwyn.

He was a rugby man through and through but that didn't blind him to other sports. He would study man-management in soccer and make trips to Old Trafford to chew the fat with people like the manager, Dave Sexton. That was where he learnt about how they gave their players the best of everything on the basis that the players would give the club their best every time they played.

Carwyn gave us the best at Llanelli. He made sure we were all happy in our environment, on the pitch and away from it. He made a point of getting to know our families so that if

Maesteg Comprehensive School athletics team 1965–6. The teenaged JJ is sitting to the right of the schoolmaster, David Brown.

The Wales Schools' team 1966 including four 17 year olds who would play for Wales – JPR sitting, second left; Keith Hughes at the end of the row on the right; JJ front, right; Allan Martin, third from the right at the back.

Beating Olympic sprinter Ron Jones to the tape, Jenner Park, Barry, 1969.

JJ (No. 11) winning the Welsh AAA's 110-yard title at Cwmbrân Stadium, 1969.

Relay rehearsal at Aberystwyth, early summer 1970, for the Wales quartet at the Commonwealth Games later that year. JJ hands the baton to Howard Davies.

© Raymond Daniel

The newlyweds – John and Jane, April 1972.

The family's two-year-old Ford Prefect in 1960. Twelve-year-old John, big brother Peter, and their mother, Lizzie.

Outside Llangunnor Church on the big day. From left: Roger Lane, Peter Williams, John, Jane, Allan Martin, David Liddington.

Another family occasion, James Williams on the day of his marriage to Imogen. From left: Richard (Peter's son), cousin Siriol, Rhys, the groom, JJ, brothers Terry and Peter, son-in-law Graham and, in front, grandson, Joshua.

JJ with Max Boyce. No scoreboard can ever have told a more enduring story than this one – Llanelli 9, All Blacks 3 at Stradey Park, October 1972.

JJ making an immediate impact on his Wales debut against France in Paris, 1973.

Preparing with Wales before the Murrayfield Sevens in 1973. Back, from left: John Taylor, Gerald Davies, Clive Rowlands, Mervyn Davies, JPR, Gareth Edwards, Glyn Shaw. Front, from left: JJ, Ian Lewis, Phil Bennett and physio Gerry Lewis.

Living the dream at Cardiff Arms Park, January 1974.

JJ training among the sand dunes at Merthyr Mawr.

Touching down for the first time in a home Test, against France at the Arms Park, February 1974.

Wales line up at Twickenham against England in 1974. JJ is in the back row next to the man who would deny him a crucial late try, Irish referee John West.

The invincible 1974 Lions in South Africa. JJ is in the front row, third from the right, taking care of the lion.

John Williams in triplicate during the Lions' series in South Africa in 1974. From left, JPR, Springbok second row John Williams, and a beaming JJ.

Lions 26, South Africa 9, and arguably JJ's most famous try, at Boet Erasmus, Port Elizabeth, July 1974.
© Colorsport

Relaxing over a braii in South Africa. From left, Chris Ralston, sitting; JJ and Tom Grace, standing; Geoff Evans and Mervyn Davies, crouching.

JJ and Scotland prop Ian McLauchlan in a celebratory hug at the end of the unbeaten tour.

Nantyffyllon welcomes its conquering hero home from the invincible Lions tour – a pony and trap for Jane and her husband, the drum majorettes on parade along Picton Street and all the civic dignitaries, July 1974.

Presenting the match ball used in one of the South Africa-Lions series to Nantyffyllon RFC chairman Paul Hughes, 1974.

Meeting with the vanquished Springbok captain, Hannes Marais in Hong Kong.

A trio of Lions training with Natal (Sharks) – JPR, Ian 'Mighty Mouse' McLauchlan, JJ; August 1975.

Wales just before their momentous 25–10 win over France at the Parc des Princes with six new caps, January 1975. Back row, from left: Graham Price, Ray Gravell, Geoff Wheel, Allan Martin, Trefor Evans, Charlie Faulkner, Terry Cobner, Steve Fenwick. Front row: JJ, John Bevan, JPR, Mervyn Davies, Bobby Windsor, Gareth Edwards, Gerald Davies.

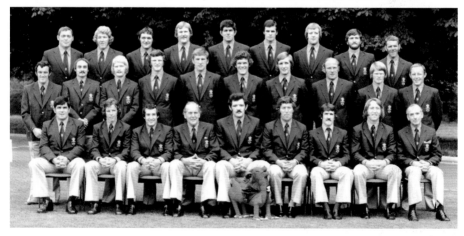

The Wales squad before taking off on their record-breaking tour of Japan in September 1975.

SPORTSMAIL EXCLUSIVE

Lions winger Williams offered £15,000 to turn professional for Widnes

BY PETER JACKSON

BRITISH LIONS wing John J. Williams has been offered £15,000 to join Widnes Rugby League Club.

The 25-year-old Maesteg schoolteacher, fresh from his record-breaking contribution to the Lions tour of South Africa, told me last night: 'I've had a big offer. At the moment it is 50-50, but I've never had an offer as tempting as this one.'

Widnes coach Vince Karalius is believed to have approached Williams in South Wales earlier this week.

The Llanelli player, the only man in British Rugby history to score four tries in a Test series in South Africa, will let Widnes know his decision tomorrow.

Williams, who also scored a record six tries in a tour match, added : 'This has come right out of the blue. I've had many offers from Rugby League clubs in the past and I always thought they would have to make a very good one to get me to leave.

'Before I just wasn't interested, but this is such a good offer that I'm still thinking about it.'

Capped six times by Wales, Williams is a physical education instructor at a Maesteg comprehensive school. He says both he and his wife could get teaching posts in the North.

Williams's decision to tour with Lions cost him nearly £500.

His application to his employers, the Mid-Glamorgan Education Authority, for three-months' paid leave was refused, partly because of the apartheid issue.

Millionaire and former Springbok Jan Pickard offered to compensate Williams for his loss of wages, but Williams refused because this would have contravened Rugby's laws about amateur players.

Widnes, I understand, have been pressing Williams for a decision, but if, as is likely, the player agrees to the move, his League debut will have to wait at least until next week.

Like most of the triumphant Lions, Williams has been taking it easy. He said : 'I've only just started training, again.

Williams played for the World XV in Ireland earlier this month but had no plans to return to competitive club Rugby until next month.

The money Widnes are prepared to pay him falls just short of the record Rugby League fee of £16,000 which Salford paid Newport for outside-half David Watkins in 1967.

Williams . . . 'I'm tempted to accept this time.'

The *Daily Mail* report of JJ's record offer from Widnes Rugby League Club. For 'considering' the offer, the WRU threatened to ban him for life for a breach of the amateur regulations.

JJ shakes hands with the mayor of Newport before joining Bobby Windsor (left) and Phil Bennett in a charity match for Newport Saracens. As a result, all three players were told by the WRU they had been banned.

Scoring for Llanelli against Cardiff at the Arms Park, 1975.

Running riot against the Wallabies, for the Barbarians at Cardiff Arms Park, January 1976.

JJ sliding over in the pouring rain on his way to a hat-trick of tries in the opening match of the Lions tour, against Wairarapa Bush in Masterton, May 1977.

A rare dry day for the Lions in the New Zealand winter of 1977. Trevor Evans, left, Ian McGeechan and JJ feeling the cold on a volcano near New Plymouth.

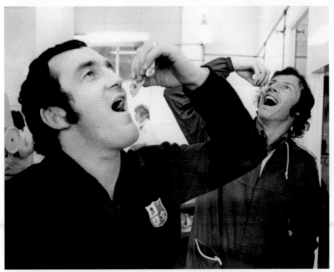

Phil Bennett and JJ sampling the local delicacies in Invercargill, oyster capital of New Zealand.

Scoring the decisive try in the Lions' victory over the All Blacks, Second Test, Lancaster Park, Christchurch, July 1977.

In the middle of two front row giants – Fran Cotton, left, and Bobby Windsor.

An all-star line-up of Cardiff College of Education (Cardiff Met.) old boys on the eve of Wales-England, March 1979. Back, from left: Clive Rowlands, Syd Aaron, Leighton Davies (both lecturers), Stuart Lane. Front: JJ, Brynmor Williams, David Richards, Clive Griffiths and Allan Martin.

On the podium at the final of *Superstars*, Cwmbrân Stadium, 1980. From left: John Sherwood, Sir Geoff Hurst, Steve Assinder, JJ, Alan Minter, Danny Nightingale, Daley Thompson, Brian Jacks.

A reunion in the WREX Room at the Millennium Stadium 2003 with three All Blacks – Earl Kirton (centre, front), directly behind him Brian Lochore and, to his right, Tane Norton.

Bernard Jones, fourth from left, presenting a cheque for £10,000 in 2010 to the WREX charity for former players. From left: Gareth Edwards, David Watkins, JPR, Bernard Jones, Mervyn Davies, JJ, Steve Fenwick, Tommy David.

JJ named in the all-time greatest Wales XV at a ceremony in Cardiff.

Trying hard to keep up with the youngsters – JJ training with, from left, James, Kathryn and Rhys.
© Paul Stuart

Rhys Williams with his dad and his first European medal, 400 metres hurdles, Gothenburg, 2006.

Rhys in Olympic action, London 2012.

Rhys after winning silver for Great Britain at the European championships in Barcelona, 2010.

Kathryn Williams, blazing the trail as the family's first GB international 400-metre hurdler.

Father and daughter in Aberdeen where Kathryn captained the Welsh schools' team.

James Williams (No. 74), a 1,500-metre runner completing the family's full set of international athletes.

JJ, television pundit, alongside commentator Huw Llywelyn Davies in Pretoria in June 1998, just before Wales lose to the Springboks by a record score, 96–13.

The Williamses at Buckingham Palace in May 2013 after JJ received his MBE from the Queen for services to rugby and charity. From left: James, Jane, JJ, Kathryn, Rhys.

JJ and Jane, 2015, relaxing at their home in Portugal.

anyone had a problem outside rugby, he would be there with some practical help. I never heard anyone say a bad word about him.

Nobody admired Carwyn more than I did but in any debate on the rights and wrongs of his non-appointment as Wales coach one question has to be asked:

Why should the WRU have changed their system just to suit Carwyn's demands? They had been successful in picking teams that won things, from Grand Slams to Sevens competitions.

Of course, Carwyn should have had the job and I've often wondered how good Wales would have been under his direction. It would have meant John Dawes waiting two or three years instead of succeeding Clive Rowlands right away but that wouldn't have been a problem because John and Carwyn were big mates. As graduates of the same school of rugby philosophy, they ought to have been some combination.

If they'd really wanted Carwyn, the Union could have reached some sort of compromise arrangement although Mr James was never one for compromise. I would not be at all surprised if he knew right from the outset that he would never be asked to coach Wales because he knew the conditions he made were unacceptable.

I'd love to have seen him running the national team. There would certainly have been more style to the game because style was one thing Carwyn had by the bucketful. The letter he wrote ruling himself out of contention also ruled him out of Welsh rugby for the rest of his days.

It is hard to find words to describe the sense of loss to the game in Britain and Ireland as a whole. He was always very much a loner and that may have contributed to his rejection.

He turned his back on British rugby when he had so much more to offer. He stood as a parliamentary candidate for Plaid Cymru in Llanelli during the 1970 General Election and his failure to win the seat would only have increased his sense of rejection.

Meanwhile, back on the field, the show went on. I discovered very quickly that doors which would otherwise have been closed were suddenly flung open to me on the strength of what I had done for the Lions in South Africa.

One such door took me to Dublin at the start of the 1974–5 season to play for the Irish President's XV against Ireland in a fixture marking the centenary of the Irish Rugby Union. Fergus Slattery and Stewart McKinney got tries for Ireland, Gareth and I replied on behalf of the President. Mike Gibson and Phil Bennett kicked four goals each and we drew the match, 18-all.

Twenty-four hours later I was making my debut for the Irish Wolfhounds invitational team against Munster for what was an experience and a half. Except for me, the Wolfhounds consisted entirely of Frenchmen and they were all getting stuck into the Guinness before the match. Some of them liked it so much they must have had three pints, not that I was counting.

The match had been billed as an exhibition and for the entire first half the French Wolfhounds lived up to the pre-match hype. They made such an exhibition of themselves that we were 30-nil down at half-time. Gareth and Phil were almost wetting themselves with laughter on the sideline.

My French is not very good but, boy, did they get a rollicking at half-time. It was given by the scrum half, Jacques Fouroux, and I could see why they likened him to Napoléon under the nickname *Le Petit General*.

Whatever threats Jacques made had the desired effect. Whether the Guinness had worn off by then I couldn't say but my 14 French *confrères* knuckled down and turned the tide so completely that we won the match 33–30.

In rugby, especially in the amateur days, the sublime was never very far from the ridiculous and vice versa. A couple of months after the Irish jaunt, in mid-November, Wales played a Test match against the All Blacks at Cardiff Arms Park on a Wednesday afternoon except that, officially, it wasn't a Test match.

The Kiwis had been on tour in Ireland to mark their centenary and for some very strange reason that didn't make sense, the WRU decided that they would not take any of the shine off the Irish by awarding caps. If they felt that strongly, why did they bother arranging the fixture in the first place and then charging the usual top price for tickets?

This is the same Union who later decided in their wisdom to give caps for matches against the Barbarians as if a country called Barbaria really existed. So it wasn't Wales that played New Zealand that day, it was a Wales XV. How pedantic can you get? And who were they kidding? Everyone knew it was a full-on Test match.

We lost 12–3; Phil Bennett, alarmingly, missed a few kicks but, worst of all, Ian Hall, the Aberavon centre, broke his ankle so badly that I remember looking at his leg and noticing that it was about three inches apart from his ankle. It was the worst injury I ever saw on a rugby field but Ian, being the dedicated player he was, fought his way back against all the odds and made a comeback but he was never the same again.

We should have been on fire for the All Blacks but we weren't. Most of us had hardly played any club rugby worth talking about after our exertions for the Lions that summer. The fixture came too soon in the season for us but it was significant in one respect because it marked the arrival of a man who would bring the necessary grunt and expertise to the front row for Wales to win two Grand Slams in three years and four Triple Crowns on the bounce.

Charlie Faulkner was his name and I'd first heard mention of him towards the end of the Lions tour a few months previously. A few of the Welsh contingent were sitting in a hotel in Durban discussing our prospects for the coming season and expressing concern at the overall state of the pack. Yes, we had Mervyn, Bobby and Tommy but where we were going to get a scrum from? That was our Achilles heel. Who was ready to step up?

And that was when Bobby said: 'Listen, I've got a boy playing with me at Pontypool. Before that we played together at Cross Keys. His name is Charlie Faulkner, he's over here and he'll be dropping in for a chat tomorrow.'

The next day, true enough, Charlie Faulkner walked into the hotel. He was the most unlikely looking international sportsman I'd ever seen. To put it politely, he did not appear to be athletic which only goes to show that looks can be very misleading.

What he did have was a marvellous attitude and a sense of humour. He also had a black belt in judo which meant he had power and strength in abundance. And he was also under the guidance of one of the all-time great props, the Pontypool coach, Ray Prosser.

And then, to everyone's surprise, Charlie made a speech. 'Gentlemen,' he said of the Pontypool front row. 'We may go up and we may go down but we never go backwards. Never.'

For backs like myself and JPR, this was music to ears. Here was someone who would make sure we had a platform to win enough ball. Absolutely fantastic, and Charlie proved to be as good as his word, including stealing a try from me when we won the Five Nations title in 1975 against Ireland at the Arms Park.

Before the All Blacks went home, I had hoped for a second crack at them in the traditional end-of-tour match against the Barbarians. This one was held at Twickenham and the Baa-baas signalled their intention by picking eight forwards from the Lions tour under the captaincy of Willie John McBride.

When the team was announced, my name wasn't there. Neither was Phil's. They picked Gerald Davies on one wing,

Peter Preece of Coventry and England on the other, even though he was a centre, and, to keep the Baa-baas tradition of always having one uncapped player, they picked John Bevan of Aberavon ahead of Phil.

Both of us were demoralised at being left out of such a prestigious fixture.

Phil was going through a very traumatic time as a result of he and Pat losing their baby. Naturally, that had a devastating effect on them. Understandably, Phil's mind really wasn't on rugby. When he didn't turn up for the final Welsh trial and squad sessions, the Big Five decided to make an example of him.

They also left him out of the team and the reserves for the opening Five Nations match against France in Paris on 18 January 1975. John Bevan made his debut and the back-up No. 10 was a 20-year-old kid from Swansea, David Richards. So Phil had suddenly gone from being the world-beating No. 1 for the Lions to, at the very best, No. 3 for Wales.

In truth, he had been his own worst enemy. The Big Five didn't like it when he cried off the trial and they liked it even less when Phil turned out for Llanelli the following Monday. The selectors had strict codes of practice and the way they saw it, they could not excuse one player and take a harder line with others.

Phil left them no excuse to do anything other than drop him. So off we went to Paris with six new caps – Ray Gravell, Steve Fenwick, John Bevan, Charlie Faulkner, Graham Price and Trefor Evans – and thrashed France 25–10. The crowning glory came in the last minute when Price got his famous try in the right-hand corner of the Parc des Princes.

I always have a joke with him about that. 'Pricey, I made that try for you by sprinting 60 metres and making the slide tackle on the full back so that the ball popped up for you to finish it off.'

Whenever I suggest to him, tongue in cheek, that it was my try, he always says: 'If you had pinched it from me, I'd have broken your f****** nose.' Typical Pontypool. No sentiment.

Prosser's reaction also typified the Pontypool philosophy. When Graham reported for training on the Monday night after Paris, Prosser took him to one side for a quiet word. 'That prop you were up against on Saturday can't have been much good,' says Prosser.

'Why not?' says Pricey.

'Because,' says Prosser. 'If he'd been any use at all you wouldn't have been able to run as far as you did for that try.'

John Bevan came of age as an international player in Paris, setting the back line moving in a slightly different way to Phil Bennett. People were beginning to criticise 'Benny' for drifting across the field as he passed. 'Bev' was more direct and while he was nowhere near as flamboyant, he had a wonderful rugby brain and his death some ten years later at the age of 38 was a tragedy for rugby in the widest sense.

Suddenly, Phil was on the outside looking in. The team that won in Paris was bound to be unchanged for the next match, England at home, and we took that in our stride with nobody any the wiser that five of us, as has been explained, were threatened with being banned for life as professionals.

I got the first of our three tries, not that it compensates in any way for the one that Mr West denied me at Twickenham the previous season. So it was on to the third leg of a possible Grand Slam, Scotland at Murrayfield, and all the new boys who'd done so well in the first two matches kept their places. Phil was still on the outside and if it hadn't been for fate taking a hand, he would probably have spent the whole of that Five Nations as just another spectator.

This was my first international in Scotland and I shall never forget the sight which greeted my eyes when I woke up that Saturday morning, drew back the curtains and looked out onto Princes Street. All I saw was a sea of red and I remember thinking to myself: 'How are they going to cope with all these fans?'

I'd never seen Welsh support for an away match on such a scale. When I read in the papers the next day that the crowd was 104,000, then the biggest for a rugby match anywhere in the world, I knew they'd all got in. And that, for obvious reasons, was the last non-ticket international played in Edinburgh.

The Scots had some players who were exceptional by any standard – Andy Irvine, Ian McGeechan, John Rutherford, 'The Mouse' (Ian McLauchlan), 'Broon frae Troon' (Gordon Brown) and Sandy Carmichael. All except Rutherford had been team-mates with the Lions the year before and that only made them more determined to put one over on the Welsh. 'The Mouse' even went as far as promising that they would give us 'hell'.

Even so we believed we had enough to win but we hadn't planned for our strategy being fractured by two horrible injuries which disrupted our midfield. Steve Fenwick broke his jaw and then John Bevan dislocated his shoulder, a blow which allowed Phil to remind the Big Five that he was still around.

As far as I was concerned, he wasn't in the right frame of mind that day. Phil would never admit that he didn't want to be there but to have been acclaimed as one of the best rugby players in the world one minute and then to have been dumped out of the Wales squad the next had shaken his confidence.

His mind was also in turmoil because of the tragedy he and Pat had gone through over losing the baby. In hindsight, he shouldn't have been there. As captain, Mervyn Davies hardly made a mistake but he made one that day at Murrayfield which he told me about years later.

Phil hadn't been on the field long when we got a penalty

well within his range and 'Merve' asked him to kick. He said that Phil refused and that Merve then ordered him to take it. He missed, just as Allan Martin missed a very difficult shot which could have won it for us.

Instead we went down 12–10 despite Trefor Evans scoring the only try of the game right at the end. The Triple Crown and the Slam had gone and the way we finished the season, running riot against Ireland at the Arms Park, ensured we won the title.

At Llanelli, we finished the season at the Arms Park with what was now becoming an annual event – the Welsh Cup final. For the second year running, we beat Aberavon to make it a hat-trick of successive victories.

My plans for a summer off were changed by a phone call from South Africa and someone we had met out there with the Lions the year before, Mr Paddy Burgess. He ran Northlands, a Durban club who played in the second division of the Natal league. He knew that, as a schoolteacher, I'd be on holiday for most of July and the whole of August.

'Why don't you come over and play for us,' he said. 'We'll put you and Jane up in a very nice hotel right beside the Indian Ocean and you can play a bit of rugby at the weekends. And we're also hoping that JPR will be playing for us as well so you'll be in good company.'

At the end of the Lions tour, JPR had stayed in Durban where he and his wife, Cilla, worked as locums in one of the hospitals. That was a brave decision on his part because Tommy Bedford, the captain of Natal, was a folk hero in Durban – the same Tommy Bedford who JPR had poleaxed when the Lions beat Natal.

With his long hair held in place by a headband, Bedford looked every inch the warrior and the fans loved him. They were roaring their heads off when he ran down the touchline, chipped ahead and JPR's late tackle almost put him into the stand. It provoked the biggest riot I have ever seen during a rugby match.

The crowd went berserk. Oranges, Coke cans and all sorts of other missiles rained down on us and while all that was going on, we took the only sensible option open to us. We went to the centre of the pitch hoping we would be out of range for all the stuff they were throwing at us. It must have taken them the best part of 15 minutes to clear the pitch and get the game going again.

It was safe to say that JPR and Durban had a bit of history. When I spoke to him about the Northlands proposal, he was really up for it, as I thought he would be and by then he and Tommy had buried the hatchet. Paddy had also got the 'Mighty Mouse' himself to come along with his wife, Eileen, and their three sons. So all of a sudden here was this junior club with three Test Lions in their ranks.

On our way to Durban, we had to change planes at Johannesburg. As Jane and I waited there, a call came over the airport tannoy: 'Would JJ Williams please report to the information centre?'

When I picked up the phone, someone from the Natal Rugby Union was on the other end, telling me that a plane was leaving in 15 minutes and could I please get on it because they wanted to introduce me to the crowd before that afternoon's Currie Cup match against Eastern Transvaal.

I said: 'Sure, no problem.'

What they didn't tell me was that there was only one seat and there were two of us. There was only one solution – Jane would have to wait for the next flight which, naturally enough, she wasn't very happy about but she agreed to stay and catch the next one a few hours later. My seat, in fact, was in the cockpit between the two pilots.

Her mood improved when she saw where we were staying, the Cabana Beach hotel at Umhlanga Rocks, an upmarket place a few miles out of Durban on the Indian Ocean. Everyday we would watch the fishermen catching barracuda in their shark nets and everyday, wherever we went, they treated us like Royalty.

I played every Saturday and did some coaching at local schools during the week. The weather was glorious, we had a car at our disposal and we were really getting into the holiday atmosphere when we met the chairman of the Natal Rugby Union. He said it would be a great honour if we would make ourselves available to play for Natal in the Currie Cup. We would be the first players from the club to achieve that distinction.

Now we were looking at a whole new ball game. From junior stuff to the Currie Cup is a huge leap. We agreed and duly turned up at Kings Park for our first training session with Natal which turned out to be the most bizarre one I'd ever experienced.

Bedford took the session and it consisted of touch rugby and nothing else. So we asked him: 'What about the moves for Saturday?' And Tommy said: 'Don't worry about it.'

Don't worry about it!

I played two Currie Cup matches for them, scored one try and lived to tell the tale. Jane and I stayed on after JPR and 'The Mouse' had gone home, long enough to return to Rorke's Drift for a coaching session with the local team. All expenses were paid and I know there were a lot of rumours to the contrary but when it came to playing, no money ever changed hands.

Believe me, no expense was spared. When I arrived late one day at Durban airport and missed the flight to Johannesburg where I was due to give a talk on South African rugby's coaching video, they said they had a test flight leaving in half an hour. As the only passengers on board, Jane and I had the whole plane to ourselves. Spooky…

Just as we were thinking about home and the start of a new term back in Wales, the director of education for Natal offered us teaching jobs in Durban. By then we'd begun to see how grim life was for the blacks under the apartheid system. We stayed once in an old colonial mansion at Rorke's Drift with a wonderful dining room and saw how the black servants were put upon and not treated as they ought to have been.

It was also made clear to us that if we accepted the teaching jobs in Durban, we would be expected to take out South African citizenship. I thought about it – for less than ten seconds. There was never any chance, even if they might have been thinking in terms of making me a Springbok. Their whole rugby culture had been shaken so badly by the Lions that it had been reduced to its lowest ebb.

We went home and no sooner had the new 1975–6 season began than I was off again, this time to Japan with Wales. None of us had been to the Far East and our first sight of Asia was of the boat people as we looked down on the harbour of Hong Kong from the window of our hotel.

The poverty was as bad as any I had seen in South Africa. Staying in one of the most luxurious hotels in the world and seeing the boat people living in squalor just across the road made us stop and think about the equality of life. It had a marked effect on my room-mate, Ray Gravell.

'Grav' was badly affected by what he saw, and he was bad enough before we got to Hong Kong! He'd decided that if he went out for a stroll round the shops in Hong Kong he would catch some terrible disease so it was a devil of a job to lift his spirits enough even to get him out of the room other than for training.

On the Friday night before our opening match against a Hong Kong XV, Paul Ogulta, a friend of Gareth Edwards from days in college in Cardiff, took three of us out for dinner with the managing director of the Hilton Hotel. Gareth, Gerald

Davies and I went to this magnificent hotel and had a convivial evening with the M.D.

We avoided all temptation to have a drink, enjoyed our meal and retired at a reasonable hour, explaining to our host that we had a big game the next day while thanking him for his hospitality. Imagine then my shock when we lined up for kick-off to find that the man marking me on the right wing for Hong Kong was none other than the Hilton Hotel M.D.

The previous night he gave us the impression that he would be attending the match for sure, but never even hinted that he would be playing in it. Had his plan been to ply us with drink, and I'm not for one moment saying it was, then it failed. We won 57–3 and then it was on to Tokyo.

Wales' manager was Les Spence of Cardiff, a very popular man who had been captured by the Japanese during the Second World War. The Japanese manager, Shiggy Konno, was a tremendous character with a wartime story of his own. He used to describe himself as a trainee kamikaze pilot.

While Les took it all in his stride with unfailing dignity and courtesy, one of my team-mates made it very clear to the rest of us that he, the player, was there to try and settle a few scores from the war.

Geoff Wheel was a man on a mission, one so important that he undertook it despite a lifelong fear of flying. His uncle had been a prisoner-of-war in the Far East and Geoff made no secret of the fact that he was going to 'sort out' a few Japenese on the field, a kind of retrospective justice on behalf of the Wheel family. Geoff had no way of knowing that the gods would conspire against him at every turn.

For his first training session in Japan, he trained in a wetsuit. The temperature was up in the high 80s and the humidity almost unbearable. Geoff did two laps of the field and collapsed. He had to be carried away suffering from heat exhaustion.

Two days later he was back in training, this time wearing nothing more than a pair of shorts and socks. He had gone from one extreme to the other and completed the session only to be declared unfit for the first match because he was too badly burnt by the sun.

Nothing was going to stop Geoff getting into the action. When he did, he caught an elbow belonging to one of the Japanese second rows and had to go off with a cut eye. You can't keep a good man down and Geoff had the satisfaction of playing in the first unofficial Test when we scored ten tries, and watching the second when we scored 14 more.

We won 82–6 when the try was still worth four points so it would have been 96–6 under the current system. Shiggy Konno tore into the Japanese team, criticising them for a lack of effort which I thought was grossly unfair. As far as I was concerned, Japan had been heroic, although the 'sorting out', as Geoff Wheel called it, had been well and truly taken care of, all within the laws of the game.

As a sign of the Welsh team's popularity, Princess Chichibu, a member of the Japanese Imperial Family, presented every player with a lovely silver pocket watch, beautifully inscribed. The princess gave the WRU a huge video camera which was so state-of-the-art that you couldn't buy it anywhere in the UK. It would have cost a fortune. And what did the WRU have up their sleeve as a reciprocal present in return for the glittering goodies? A tie.

Well, that must have stretched someone's imagination to breaking point. We had seen that happen so often that we were no longer embarrassed by it. The mind boggles at what our gracious Japanese hosts thought of it but they were, of course, far too polite to have suggested that the exchange of gifts seemed every bit as one-sided as the results of the matches.

'Grav' helped himself to three tries but it didn't improve

his mood. He spent every day in fear that some disease would leap out of nowhere and kill him. He survived and even came home with the pocket watch. We were half-expecting the WRU to take them all from us on the basis that they exceeded the £50 limit or whatever it was for the value of gifts. Had they done so, I'd like to think we'd have been strong enough as a group to have told them where to go…

CHAPTER 8

Grand Slam supreme

Peter Jackson

AT THE START of the 2015 Rugby World Cup, a grand total of 130 players had held the distinction of captaining Wales – an average lifespan of 12 months give or take a day or two here and there. More than a few learnt the rudiments of the game in England, among them arguably the most successful one of all.

Mervyn Davies stands out from such glittering company as unique, if only because he went from the comparatively genteel surrounds of Old Guildfordians to the international arena within a period of six months. He made it not because of the Welsh system but in spite of it, perennial anonymity forcing him to try his luck in the backwaters of the English game.

'I still don't know to this day how I managed it,' he told me once. 'I won no rugby honours at school, mainly because I went to an unfashionable school (Penlan Comprehensive). I played in the trials but never had a look-in, probably because our teachers were not on the selection committee. I played a bit of college rugby and one game for Swansea before going to London.

'I lived in Guildford for a few months and during that time a couple of mates came up with the idea of going to play for the local club, Old Guildfordians. The standard was desperately bad, almost to the point of being horrendous. So we decided to make the long journey in those non-motorway days from Guildford to London Welsh.

'I began in the third team, the London Welsh Dragons. The following Saturday, I was up to the second team, the London Welsh Druids. I thought: This is a bit more like it – some half-decent rugby.

'The half-term holiday then intervened and I drove back to Swansea to see my parents. A telegram arrived a couple of days later to say I'd been chosen for the London Welsh first team to play Moseley. That was in the November and by the third week of January I was playing for Wales. I thought: This is too easy. Nobody really knew who I was or where I'd come from. I felt it couldn't happen that quickly.'

His career, he would tell you with disarming modesty, had been a series of lucky breaks. While he may have fitted perfectly into the identikit image of the buccaneering rugby warrior, Davies' every move on the field, every thought in his head, revolved around winning as opposed to entertaining.

John Dawes, his friend from the days when London Welsh were the most admired team in British rugby, always wanted to win with style. For Davies, the physical duel dominated a philosophy which he articulated under three, one-word categories – confrontation, consolidation, domination.

As captain, Davies could be brutally honest and castigate himself when he thought the occasion demanded it. He never skirted around the truth by uttering the mumbo-jumbo of modern players afraid to say anything lest it would cause a smidgen of offence. Far from 'taking the positives', he often traded in taking the biggest negative he could find and shaking it by the throat.

For example, he blamed himself for ordering Phil Bennett to take a shot at goal against Scotland shortly after appearing as a replacement. When Bennett decided, for whatever reason, that he wasn't up for it, his captain pulled rank. The penalty attempt failed, Scotland won by two points and Davies readily acknowledged that his refusal to recognise that his goal-kicker was not in the right frame of mind had cost his country a Grand Slam.

JJ

MERVYN DAVIES LAID it on the line at our first team meeting of the campaign in September 1975. 'Boys,' he said to us. 'We've got seven matches this season which is three more than usual. I expect us to win them all. If we want to be remembered in the history of the game, we *have* to win them all. Seven out of seven.'

We looked at one another as if we were all thinking the same thing: 'That's asking a lot.' It would have been stretching a point to have referred to the Japan games as 'Tests' but they were international matches and the schedule after that would get progressively more difficult – Australia, England, Scotland, Ireland and France.

That brought personal challenges on a bigger scale than before and not just on the field because the new season came with a new job. I left teaching and went into the pharmaceutical business, selling pills and tablets to the medical professional. My change of employment with Sandoz meant I'd be rejoining forces with a very familiar figure who just happened to be on the same payroll.

Clive Rowlands was more than another rep. He was the most successful in the whole of the company. It did not take me long to discover the secret of his success and how he went about the job from his home in the Swansea Valley.

Clive had every doctor for miles around eating out of the palm of his hand, or, to be more accurate, the palms of both hands at the same time. He would only have to walk into any surgery within a wide radius of his home in Upper Cwmtwrch and the doctor would clear his desk to see him and, no doubt, seek his views on the hot rugby issue of the day.

We had an area manager, Ken Matthews, who did everything for Clive, from helping him pronounce some of the more tongue-twisting names of the drugs to explaining their function. Other reps, many of them highly educated, found themselves a long way behind in Clive's slipstream. What puzzled them more than anything was how he found the time to get round to a whole regiment of doctors over a large area and see them all. So Ken called him one day.

'Clive,' he says. 'We've been having some complaints from some of the other reps, all asking me: How the hell does Clive Rowlands do it so much better than the rest of us?'

'I told them I didn't know. I told Clive that it was important that when he saw the doctor, he left a calling card.'

Nothing more was said for a fortnight or so. Ken then calls Clive again and says: 'How many doctors have you seen this week?'

'Between 20 and 30,' says Clive.

According to Ken, Clive then reeled off the names. The word got out and when I next bumped into him, I asked him how on earth he'd found the time to see so many.

'Simple,' he says. 'I was at St Helen's for the Swansea match on Wednesday night and I was back there on the Saturday afternoon. I saw Dr Smith, Dr Thomas, Dr Jones, Dr Griffiths, Dr Williams – they were all in the stand on Wednesday night.

'And I saw them all there again on Saturday along with Dr Evans, Dr Lewis, Dr Rowlands and quite a few other Dr Joneses. I saw them, didn't I?'

They didn't call him 'Top Cat' for nothing. His sales technique was second to none. I didn't try to compete with him, using most of my free time to run up and down the sandhills at Merthyr Mawr near Porthcawl where Jane and I were living at the time.

I'd get back from work at midday, jump over the garden fence and start attacking the sand dunes. The change of job meant a change of training routine and, with a lot more heavy work designed to increase power and endurance. Slowly, it began to dawn on me that the power stuff was affecting my pace, with slow being the operative word.

People had noticed, apparently, and they were not slow in coming forward to ask questions about whether I was losing my pace. A few went as far as to wonder whether I was still worth my place in the Wales team. Clive Rees, my fellow Lion in South Africa the year before, was breathing down my neck.

The whispers were rumbling around in the run-up to the first Test of the season, Australia at the Arms Park on 20 December 1975.

The Wallabies were on the up, better than they had been, if still some way short of the team they became from the 1980s onward. They had some world-class players like Paul McLean at full back, John Hipwell at scrum half and Greg Cornelsen and Tony Shaw in the back row.

The third match of their tour brought them to Stradey the day before Guy Fawkes' night which gave us a close-up view of what to expect with the international in mind. The Australians began their trip with a romp over Oxford University only to lose to Cardiff three days later.

We had every reason, therefore, to fancy our chances of taking another Southern Hemisphere scalp to put alongside the one we'd taken at New Zealand's expense three years earlier. We had even more reason to think we would complete the most unusual of Antipodean doubles when we were leading 28–16 with not much more than a quarter of an hour left on the clock.

Norman Gale had succeeded Carwyn James as coach and it seemed like business as usual, another opportunity for Llanelli to show everyone on the rugby planet that we were still world-class. I managed to score a long-range try from almost the length of the field which was as good an example as any of my trademark.

I put a speculative kick down the tramline close to touch, the ball bounced up into my hands and I had a clear run from about halfway. Andy Hill, always prolific on the opposite wing, got our other try but, in the end, they weren't quite enough to get us home. McLean inspired the Wallabies with his running, handling and place-kicking and his last penalty about three minutes from time completed a finish as amazing as the score, 28–28.

They came back to Wales at the end of the month to beat a Swansea team captained by Merve, then lost to Scotland at Murrayfield. So when they lined up in front of more than 50,000 at the Arms Park five days before Christmas, we knew we had the beating of them. We didn't think we would do it by a record score.

The rumours that I'd lost a bit of pace had refused to go away. I'd always prided myself in being able to do something magical and pull the proverbial rabbit out of the hat when the chips were down. I'd changed my training, shifting the emphasis away from power and back to sprints. I gave the sand dunes a wide berth so when the day of the Wallaby match dawned I did not need anyone to tell me that I was playing for my place.

I went out and did something no Welsh player had ever done – I scored a hat-trick of tries against Australia. Since the end of the Second World War only one player had scored more for Wales in a full international and that was Maurice Richards who got four against England at the Arms Park in 1969.

I'd scored a few hat-tricks in my time, including the double one for the Lions against South-West Districts at Mossel Bay the year before. A hat-trick for Wales meant I'd achieved another of my goals. Against Australia, with the Arms Park overflowing with festive spirit, I was lucky enough to live the dream.

All three of my tries came in the second half. A burst by Ray Gravell and quick hands from John Bevan enabled me to score the first in the corner. Gareth's garryowen and smart work from Steve Fenwick made the second and Trefor Evans started the move for the third which I finished off with my special chip-and-chase.

I was flying again and from that day until I retired, nobody ever doubted my right to be in the team. The Wallabies played some wonderful rugby on that tour without any luck at all. The best example of that came towards the end of their last match, the traditional finale against the Barbarians back at the Arms Park.

Ironically, I was the fortuitous beneficiary. The Baa-Baas did Australia the honour of picking a fantastic back division – Andy Irvine at full back, Gerald Davies on one wing, me on the other, Ray Gravell, and the great Mike Gibson at centre with a half-decent pair at half back – Gareth Edwards and Phil Bennett.

For all the big names, the Wallabies were ahead with time running out when Gordon Brown, probably out of desperation, threw a long pass out in midfield to me. I made a mess of catching it and knocked on – only by a yard or so! I picked it up at the second attempt, conscious as always of the old adage about always playing to the referee's whistle.

The whistle never came. Georges Domercq, the Frenchman in charge, didn't blow and I was on my way past two Aussie threequarters to score between the posts. Monsieur Domercq had a reputation for being fairly liberal in his interpretation of the laws but this was exceptional even by his standards.

I don't know how he missed it and I was definitely not going to stop and tell him. I'd been robbed of one try at Twickenham the year before so the way I figured it, this partly evened up the score, not that a bucketful of tries could ever compensate for the one at HQ which deprived us of victory over England.

The Aussies complained bitterly, just as I had done during the England game, but to no avail. I knew how they felt. Some were disgruntled at the after-match banquet, a case of whingeing Wallabies, although there was no disputing that they had a case. They must have been sick and tired of me because during that tour I scored five tries against them, albeit that the last one was a teeny-weeny bit fortuitous!

We might have known that pay-back time would not be long in coming but, by the time it did, we had won two Grand Slams in three seasons. We got the first at the end of the 1976 Five Nations and I regard that team as the best Wales team of the post-war era if not the best of all time, a big statement but one I believe to be absolutely justified.

It was also in one of the best international teams of all time, good enough, in my opinion, to stand comparison with the England team that won the World Cup in 2003 as well as some of the great All Black teams. Wales in 1976 had everything, an all-singing, all-dancing outfit capable of winning in whatever manner the circumstances demanded.

As captain, Mervyn was a colossus. We had everything, starting in the front row with the hardness of the Pontypool trio, Charlie Faulkner, Bobby Windsor and Graham Price, expert technicians and never less than completely ruthless. No wonder they called them the 'Viet Gwent'.

Our second row – Geoff Wheel and Allan Martin – were as good a pair of locks as any in the game. Martin was such a master of stealth that we nicknamed him 'Panther' and he was also the last of a rare breed, the toe-end, torpedo-style, long-range goal-kicking second row forward.

In the back row we had Merve flanked by a real hard-as-nails character, Terry Cobner and Trefor Evans, certainly underrated but good enough to keep a British Lion like Tommy David on the bench. Trefor was that good.

Behind the pack we had world-beaters like Gareth, Phil, Gerald and JPR. At centre we had the ultimate crash-ball expert in Ray Gravell and outside him Steve Fenwick, not the flashiest of centres, nor the quickest but his footballing brain invariably meant he was at least one step ahead of the opposition. And the fella on the other wing wasn't bad either.

We could rely, almost without exception, on someone to come up with a match-winning piece of brilliance, somehow, somewhere. Whenever we were caught in a tight corner, we nearly always had a get-out-jail card. It really was a team for all seasons, capable of doing whatever was required.

We could grind out the wins as we did in the first match of the 1976 tournament against England – 9–6 at Twickenham with three Bennett penalties to two from Alastair Hignell. Then, when the mood took us and the creative juices were flowing, we would use the full width of the pitch and run riot.

That was never better illustrated than in the third leg of the '76 Grand Slam, the Triple Crown match at Lansdowne Road. There was only one point in it until fairly late in the second half and even when Bennett kicked two penalties, Ireland were still in the game, trailing 16–9.

What happened next was probably the most purple of patches in the history of the championship. We scored three tries in such rapid succession, so that the next thing the home team knew was that they were staring at a scoreboard which read: Ireland 9, Wales 34.

Gareth, Gerald and Phil all touched down and Phil converted all three. We had scored 18 points in five minutes and turned a close match into a landslide victory. In those five minutes we found a perfection which resulted in the Irish being destroyed in front of their own fans.

People still marvel at some of the tries we created, all executed at high speed. To have been top dogs in an era when France were a frightening force was a revealing indication of how good we were. France then had threequarters who stood deep and who would cut you to ribbons with their sublime passing and angles of running.

When they tackled you, they rattled your bones more than anyone else – and that was just the backs. The French front five of that era was overflowing with menace. Gérard Cholley, Alain Paco, Robert Paparemborde, Alain Estève and Michel Palmié would beat opponents up and they weren't fussy how they went about it.

Windsor would always regale us with stories of the dirty stuff, of what went on in the scrum and how Estève's fist would come through from the second row and smash into Bobby's unprotected face. I saw it for myself on one occasion in Paris, thankfully from a safe distance out on the wing.

I remember clearly peering through the tunnel between the front rows, watching Jacques Fouroux feed the scrum and the blows come through from the second row and landing on Windsor. We all complained to the referee, Alan Hosie of Scotland, but he did nothing about it. He dismissed every complaint with the stock phrase: 'Get on with the game.'

European rugby these days is not of the highest standard. You only have to look at the three Welsh Grand Slam teams of 2005, 2008 and 2012 to see my point because all three lost nearly every match they played against New Zealand, South Africa and Australia. France in the mid-1970s were up with New Zealand and Wales as the three best teams in the world.

Shrewd observers of the game in other countries praised us as an exceptional team. They didn't come any shrewder than Mike Gibson, and the great Irish centre-cum-outside half-cum-wing paid us the highest compliment of all. He said Wales in 1976 were as good as the Lions of 1971 and he was in a perfect position to judge, as a 1971 Lion and one who was also on the receiving end of what we produced at Lansdowne Road five years later.

In beating Australia, England, Scotland, Ireland and France, we scored 15 tries and conceded two – both to France in the Grand Slam decider. Until then our try count for the four previous matches read 14 to nil. All we conceded were nine penalties – one to Australia, three to England, two to Scotland, three to Ireland.

We were the first team to top 100 points in a Five Nations season. Other records fell like autumn leaves. Gareth became the most-capped Welsh player, Phil beat his own record for the most points in a season, Merve overtook Denzil Williams as the most-capped Welsh forward and the untouchable JPR went past the legendary Billy Bancroft as the most-capped Welsh full back.

There was another incredible statistic which tends to be overlooked whenever people look back on that season. Over the course of the five Tests, we used only 17 players. We made one change to the starting XV all season – on the wing where Gerald Davies returned for the Five Nations instead of Clive Rees after missing the Wallaby match.

The other change, a substitution forced by injury, saw Mike Knill, the Cardiff tighthead, make his one and only appearance as a replacement for Graham Price. It had to be bad for any of the Pontypool front row to leave the field and Graham claimed he could not see where he was going or what he was doing because he had been gouged.

The 13 who played in every match that season were JPR, Ray Gravell, Steve Fenwick, John Bevan, Gareth Edwards, Charlie Faulkner, Bobby Windsor, Allan Martin, Geoff Wheel, Terry Cobner, Mervyn Davies, Trefor Evans and myself.

Just look at the Wales record in 1976:

20 December 1975: beat Australia at Cardiff Arms Park, 28–6.
Tries: JJ 3, Edwards; Conversions: Fenwick 2, Martin;
Penalty: Fenwick; Drop goal: Bevan.

17 January 1976: beat England at Twickenham, 21–9.
Tries: JPR 2, Edwards; Conversions: Fenwick 3; Penalty: Martin.

7 February 1976: beat Scotland at Cardiff Arms Park, 28–6.
Tries: JJ, Edwards, Evans; Conversions: Bennett 2;
Penalties: Bennett 3; Drop goal: Fenwick.

21 February 1976: beat Ireland at Lansdowne Road, 34–9.
Tries: G Davies 2, Edwards, Bennett; Conversions: Bennett 3;
Penalties: Bennett 3, Martin.

6 March 1976: beat France at Cardiff Arms Park, 19–13.
Try: JJ; Penalties: Bennett 2, Fenwick 2, Martin.

We were on top of the world. We didn't have the World Cup because there wasn't one. Had there been, it would have been a three-horse race – New Zealand, France, Wales. In addition to proving ourselves undisputed champions of Europe, our best players had played decisive roles for the Lions in their successive tour victories over New Zealand and South Africa.

The sky really was the limit. Merve said so himself straight after the France game. When the reporters asked him what was next for Wales, the skipper deliberately set the bar higher than ever. 'Three Grand Slams in a row,' he said. And we all, to a man, believed him. We might have been up in the clouds that weekend as the whole nation celebrated our success but our journey had really only begun.

Three Grand Slams in a row had never been done. England in the 1920s won it three times in four seasons, as had Wales a decade earlier, but three in three had proved beyond the very best teams in the long history of the Five-Six Nations, as it still does. We believed we had everything required to be the first.

As a team, we were winning titles for fun. We knew we were the best in Europe and that only France could live with us. The more we won, the greater the pressure we were under to keep winning and that pressure built as much from within the camp as from the public at large. Merve said what he said about winning three Slams on the bounce not as a throwaway line but because he knew we had the potential to deliver just that.

He was still mastering the art of captaincy so you wonder what more Wales could have achieved under his direction. He believed that we were only at the start of a journey which would take us to places where no international team had gone before.

A measure of how good he was can be gained from his CV as a Lion. Only the chosen few become Test Lions and fewer still belong in the most exclusive category of all as stars of series victory in New Zealand and South Africa. Mervyn Davies belonged to that rarest of breed.

Against the All Blacks in 1971, the great New Zealander, Colin Meads, singled out Merve's role at the tail of the line-out as a decisive factor in the Lions' victory. Pick your best Lions team of all time and I suggest there'd only be one choice at No. 8 – TM Davies.

He had, as we found out later, been offered the captaincy of the Lions in New Zealand the following year. The rest of the Wales team would still be at their peak for another two years, at the very least. The future couldn't have been rosier.

We were not to know that our leader would never play for Wales again. Exactly 22 days after winning the Slam he was back at the Arms Park playing for Swansea against Pontypool in the other semi-final of the Welsh Cup. We at Llanelli had won our semi against Ebbw Vale before a crowd of 20,000 at St Helen's the day before, so I had a vested interest in watching the Sunday match to find out who we'd be facing in the final.

What I saw on television was Merve collapsing without anyone near him. It looked serious but we didn't have a clue how serious until the next day. Mervyn Davies, our indestructible captain, had been cut down by a brain haemorrhage. He was at death's door.

The terrible reality was not that he would never play again but whether he would pull through. He did, of course, although he would never be quite the same again. A wonderful new era had dawned for Welsh rugby and in the days and weeks after Merve's collapse it felt as though our hopes had been struck by a thunderbolt.

To say it was a massive blow sounds now almost a bit of an understatement.

When he came out of hospital, he was a shadow of his former self. While everyone was mightily relieved that he was on the long road to recovery, it was hard to recognise him with his shaven head and hollow appearance. What mattered above all was that he was alive, thanks to the prompt attention he got at the Arms Park and the skill of the neurosurgeon, Mr Robert Weekes.

Life goes on and soon attention turned to how Wales would cope without their stricken leader. Derek Quinnell filled the huge gap in the back row. Fine player though he undoubtedly was, Derek was not Mervyn Davies, never could be. As well as a new No. 8, Wales had to find a new captain. Phil Bennett was the obvious choice to do for Wales what he was then doing for the Scarlets.

The cost of losing Merve when he was at the height of his power extended beyond changing the Welsh back row and passing the armband onto Phil. Although he was a quiet man by nature, he was a leader, an astute tactician who controlled the game like all the best outside-halves do.

The Lions paid a heavy price for Merve having been cut down in his prime. They lost a Test series against the All Blacks they ought to have won and, in my opinion, would have won had Merve been there. That is not a criticism of Phil who acknowledged a long time ago that he regretted accepting the captaincy.

He found it tough for all sorts of reasons but mostly because of the politics of the tour. He got worn down as much by the internal bickering and the breakdown of relations with the press as by the mud and rain.

Merve would have risen above the politics. He was a close friend of John Dawes and he would not have been shy about telling his old London Welsh team-mate where he was going wrong. He would have been the strong on-field commander that Dawes, as coach, needed.

In addition to all that, the Lions missed Mervyn Davies the player. Willie Duggan of Ireland did a good job but Merve was a step up again. We never quite got round to winning the Grand Slam hat-trick, settling instead for two in three years. France in Paris in 1977 wrecked the grand plan but who is to deny that had Merve been there, we'd have won the Slam that year as well?

I got a lot closer to him in later life than I had when we were playing for Wales and the Lions. I'd been instrumental in setting up the Welsh Former International Players' Association (WREX) and, as a way of getting Merve back into the game, I cleared the way for him to become our chairman.

Always fiercely independent and very much his own man, he would have played down the significance of the appointment. There's no doubt it got him back into circulation and onto the after-dinner speaking circuit. JPR told me he was seriously worried about Merve's health after he had been on stage with him at a function in London in November 2011.

Ominously, he stopped coming to the WREX room at the Millennium Stadium on the occasion of home internationals. When I went down to see him at his home in Swansea before Christmas that year, he was in a bad way, in constant need of morphine to kill the pain. He told me then: 'I haven't got long to go.'

It was desperately sad to see this wonderful athlete and supreme rugby player in the grip of such a cruel cancer. He went quickly in the end, passing away on 15 March 2012. His funeral was very low key with only his close family invited.

Two days later Wales won the Grand Slam and there was a striking poignancy to the result. They beat France 16–9 in the decider and when we went to Paris in 1977 for the first time without our captain, they beat us by the same score.

Merve would have liked the sense of history in the turning of the tables.

In the days and weeks after his private funeral, a few of us thought he deserved a slightly better send-off, that someone of his huge stature justified a memorial service. Derek Quinnell and I set about organising the event which was held at the Brangwyn Hall in Swansea, a venue with the capacity and grandeur which made it the perfect venue.

The place was packed as the rugby community paid homage to one of the greatest. The Upper Cwmtwrch choir, led by Clive Rowlands, sang Mervyn's favourite songs from his two Lions tours – 'Sloop John B' (New Zealand, 1971) and 'Flower of Scotland' (South Africa, 1974).

They came from near and far to remember him. Among those from outside Wales, Ian McLauchlan came from Scotland, Willie John McBride from Ireland and Mike Burton from England, ensuring that all four home countries were represented. And the All Blacks were represented by who else but the legendary Bryan 'Bee Gee' Williams. In his capacity as president of the New Zealand Rugby Union, he rose wonderfully to the occasion with a solo rendition of a Maori love song which brought the house down.

Mervyn would have loved it.

CHAPTER 9

Stitched up!

Peter Jackson

OF ALL THE Lions in all the world, only one has scored more tries in Tests against the Southern Hemisphere superpowers than John James Williams. His five in seven matches puts him second on the all-time list behind arguably the most charismatic Irishman ever to set foot on the international stage.

Tony O'Reilly finished with six tries from ten Tests which puts him on the top of a very distinguished pile, even if an inferior strike rate makes him look a bit of a slouch compared to the sharpest of his Welsh successors on the wing.

Capped by Ireland at the age of 18 and picked by the Lions shortly after he turned 19, O'Reilly had reached his early 20s when he reputedly turned down the offer of an audition for the title role in *Ben Hur*. Instead of making it big in Hollywood, the customs officer's son from Dublin made it even bigger in another arena of American life.

As chief executive officer and later chairman of the food conglomerate, HJ Heinz, O'Reilly became one of the most successful figures in US business. He moved in circles that made him a frequent visitor to the White House where he played tennis with George Bush Snr before and after his inauguration as the 41st President of the United States of America.

In his 38 matches for the Lions during two tours in the 1950s, O'Reilly scored 38 tries. Over the course of the 20th century, JJ got closest to his total with 22 tries from 26 appearances. The only other Lion to have scored more, the Cambridge University, Blackheath and England centre Randolph Aston (31 tries from 20 matches) got them in South Africa in 1891.

In a four-Test series, O'Reilly never managed more than two tries – against the Springboks in 1955 and against the All Blacks four years later. JJ scored twice as many in successive matches against South Africa in 1974, a feat that had never been done before, nor since.

Another Welshman, Willie Llewellyn from Tonypandy, got four in a three-match series against Australia in 1904. The following year he helped Wales beat New Zealand, the only defeat inflicted on Dave Gallaher's 'originals' during their first British tour.

The last survivor of that team, Llewellyn, a pharmacist by profession, died in Pontyclun at the age of 95 in March 1973. He was still alive when David Duckham took off with the Lions for New Zealand and landed in the record books as the first player to score six tries in one fixture.

Duckham got them in Match No. 10 of the triumphant 1971 tour, against a combined West Coast and Buller team on a very wet mid-June day in Greymouth, an old coal and gold mining town on South Island. The England wing was not supposed to be playing, let alone running riot in a manner not seen before.

He came in as an eleventh-hour replacement for John Spencer after his English compatriot strained a hamstring, an emergency to which Duckham responded by scoring five times in the first 32 minutes. His sixth, early in the second half, raised the possibility that he would eclipse the world record of eight set by the late Rod Heeps against Northern New South Wales during the All Black tour of Australia in 1962.

While the rugby world wondered whether anyone would ever equal Duckham's extravaganza, JJ Williams wasted little time coming up with the answer on his first Lions tour, to South Africa three years later. He duly emulated the Coventry wing's feat with a double hat-trick of his own against South-West Districts at Mossel Bay.

JJ's feats for the best of British and Irish are all the more commendable considering the forward-dominated approach to the 1977 series in New Zealand. The Lions managed a paltry three tries in the four Tests and of those three, only one came from the threequarters – JJ in the victory at Lancaster Park, Christchurch.

In doing so he became the first Welshman to score tries against every one of the other seven foundation members of the International Rugby Board – Australia, England, France, Ireland, New Zealand, Scotland and South Africa, a global set completed within a three-year period from 1974 and 1977.

Mervyn Davies had been offered the captaincy of the 1977 Lions in strict privacy by John Dawes a few weeks before his near-fatal brain haemorrhage. Once the Welshman and his white bandana had been so cruelly removed from the battle ground, the Lions lost another outstanding back row forward and captaincy candidate in Roger Uttley. A back injury eliminated the rugged Lancastrian from Blackpool shortly before departure, another blow to a squad that had, as events would prove, taken a few too many.

JJ

THE LIONS LOST the 1977 series in New Zealand because they made one grave error after another. They made the first one before they left by picking far too many Welsh players – 17 out of a squad of 30. Some were not good enough, others were picked ahead of their time.

The second grave error was the omission of the redoubtable Scottish Lion, Ian McLauchlan. Nobody could understand why the selectors left the 'Mighty Mouse' at home, unless it was because they considered him too strong a personality, on and off the field. Whatever the reason, they missed his destructive presence from start to finish.

Sadly, the grave errors didn't end there. Maybe the gravest of all revolved around the Lions' failure to pick Mike Gibson for any of the four Tests. They didn't just leave him out. They ignored him and we're talking here about one of the greatest threequarters of all time. His experience alone would have been priceless, yet Mike was never considered for the Test team.

Other massive selection mistakes were made. The overall impact contributed to letting the All Blacks off the hook after we had won the second of the four Tests. We should then have gone on to win the series 3–1. Instead, we managed to lose it by the same score and the tour ranks as the biggest regret of my entire career.

The '71 Lions, still the only ones to have beaten the Kiwis in New Zealand, were always going to be a hard act to follow. Instead of giving them a double dose of what had happened six years earlier, we made the act ten times more difficult. When the All Blacks were on their knees, when they reacted to losing the second Test by dropping Sid Going, a national icon, we allowed them to get back up off the ropes and take the decision.

When you make as many wrong decisions as the Lions hierarchy did on that tour, you can hardly expect anything else. Despite the daily problem of kit soaked by rain and caked in mud, we went into the last fixture before the first Test with a clean record of eight wins from eight matches.

New Zealand Universities at a packed Lancaster Park in Christchurch gave us a final warm-up before we ran into the

All Blacks in Wellington. We lost heavily, 21–9, thanks largely to some of the most one-eyed refereeing I have ever had the misfortune to witness. Sitting in the stand, I could hardly believe my eyes. We got penalised for anything and everything. It was a typically disgusting New Zealand ploy to unsettle us on the Tuesday before the Test on the Saturday.

The more serious damage was done on the Wednesday, self-inflicted by our own management. John Dawes subjected us to a training session of murderous intensity which went on and on for approximately two hours – two hours of non-stop torture.

Dawes was extremely angry that we had lost to the Universities. You could tell from his body language that this session was designed as a form of punishment. There was a river outside the hotel and beyond the far bank, a large expanse of about ten rugby fields.

He began by ordering a fast stride to the trees which were so far away that they seemed like a cluster of dots in the distance. When we weren't running to the trees and back, he had us doing press-ups, sit-ups and circuit training. By the time he eventually called a halt, we were all totally and utterly exhausted.

Some of the boys decided not to jog the long way back to the hotel via the bridge but wade across the river instead so they could get to their rooms quicker for a lie-down. The session was so counter-productive that after travelling to Wellington on the Thursday, my legs were still so stiff on the Friday that I could hardly run.

This was no way to prepare for a Test match. John's idea of fitness training was nowhere near as good as his rugby knowledge. Rugby still hadn't invented any such animal as the fitness coach so for our first clash with the All Blacks, instead of being in peak condition, our energy levels had been drained.

Despite the handicap, we had the match won and then we threw it away, literally. The chance to land a sledgehammer psychological blow on the All Blacks disappeared when the excellent Trefor Evans broke the line and passed to Andy Irvine for a try that would have put the match out of the Kiwis' reach.

Unfortunately, the ball never got to Andy. Grant Batty intercepted it instead and ran three-quarters of the length of the field for the intercept try that got the All Blacks out of jail. We had allowed them to turn a 10–12 defeat into a 16–12 win.

All of a sudden we had been beaten twice in five days. We'd paid a high price for the wake-up call and the management responded to the alarm bells by making changes. Cotton, inexplicably left out of the first Test, came in and Billy Beaumont, who had joined us as a replacement after Nigel Horton had broken his hand, went straight into the second row.

One of our major weaknesses had been an inability to win possession from re-starts. Beaumont provided an immediate solution to that problem and gave us a platform. The pack had to be shaken up but in doing so they made another grave error, this time in dropping Windsor. To this day, I cannot understand why.

Maybe the selectors thought Bobby was struggling with a calf strain but he was such a ruthless competitor that I would always have picked him. Instead the Lions preferred the English hooker Peter Wheeler, a developing player who proved himself a worthy Lion on a subsequent tour.

After the farce on the training ground before the Wellington Test, the coaching changed dramatically. Terry Cobner stepped out of the ranks to take charge of the pack and he did so in true Pontypool fashion, putting a heavy emphasis on rucking the All Blacks out of the second Test at Lancaster Park.

It had an immediate effect in getting us back to winning ways at the Test venue and settling an old score against Canterbury. Time had done nothing to heal the gaping wounds caused when the Lions were beaten up by the same provincial opposition six years before.

We all knew the gory details, how the Scottish prop, Sandy Carmichael, was given such a hammering that he had his cheekbone broken in several places as well as other facial injuries. No wonder they called them 'The Canterbury Butchers'.

In drawing up the fixture list, the Kiwis made sure that the Canterbury match fell between the first and second Tests, no doubt with a view to another exercise in softening the Lions up. If the visitors considered that what passed for a rugby match justified another X-certificate, all the better.

This time, under Cobner's leadership and with John Bevan at outside half, we met fire with fire and sorted them out up front. I found a couple of scraps and managed to turn one of them into a try and we edged it, 14–13. 'Cob' was turning the pack into a real force which they demonstrated again by taking another major provincial scalp in Wellington.

That all galvanised the pack into a formidable unit and if it meant the backs living off a starvation diet, well we had enough ability to turn the odd morsel into a delicious try. There was no question that Cobner had the forwards fired up in general and Cotton in particular.

He turned to me in the changing room just before kick-off. 'You know what we're going to do today?' Fran asked, not that I had much of a clue. 'We're going to make history, that's what we're going to do because no Lions side has ever won the second Test in Christchurch.'

Fran turned out to be something of a prophet, and I was thrilled to lend a hand with the winning try on top of Bennett's three penalties which got us home 13–9. The try, my fifth for the Lions in Tests, was one of my very best, a sweeping move covering most of the pitch. I finished it off in a way that gave me more satisfaction than any other kick and chase. This time I dummied my way past the last All Black standing between me and the line, and the fact that his name was Sid Going made it all the more satisfying. Three years earlier at Stradey, after Llanelli had beaten New Zealand, he'd told me to piss off. What goes around, comes around.

Sometimes I scored tries when the tackling was non-existent. What made this one so precious was that it won a match of huge intensity and levelled the series. The tour was back on track even if I did have some reservations. The main concern gnawing away at the back of my mind was that we were becoming too forward-orientated to the exclusion of almost everything else.

With Derek Quinnell picked on the blindside of the back row instead of Evans, and Gordon Brown in for Moss Keane, only three of the pack picked for the first Test kept their places – Graham Price at tighthead along with Cobner and the Irishman, Willie Duggan, in the back row. Brutal was hardly the word for a fierce encounter.

We had four matches before the third Test in Dunedin. We won them all and saved our biggest win for the last of the four, thrashing Auckland 34–15 at Eden Park. And then we ran headlong into another grave error. Again, we only had ourselves to blame.

For reasons best known to themselves, the tour organisers had given us a few days off before our third date with the All Blacks. There was nothing wrong except that it meant travelling from one end of New Zealand to the other, from the tropical warmth of the Bay of Islands at the top of North Island to the ice cold of Dunedin towards the bottom of South Island.

There was no value in that break whatsoever. We had

a Test series to win and we should have kept the pressure on ourselves, especially since the All Blacks appeared to have been reduced to a state of panic by their defeat in Christchurch. They did the unthinkable and dropped their No. 1 icon, Sid Going.

They replaced him at scrum-half with Lyn Davis and that signalled a big change in tactics, away from their narrow game built around the rucks and mauls. Instead they intended to play a more open game, so making more use of Bruce Robertson and Bill Osborne at centre and the great Bryan 'Bee Gee' Williams on the wing.

It had taken a huge effort and an awful lot of sweat for the Lions to gain the upper hand. It took us only a minute or so to lose it due to our failure to cope with a kick from Robertson and before we knew what had hit us Ian Kirkpatrick went over for the opening try.

Brynmor Williams' break made an equalising try for Duggan; Andy Haden then got another for the Blacks and we found ourselves six points down. The recovery operation suddenly got a whole lot tougher when injuries forced us to make changes either side of half-time.

I damaged a thigh muscle around the half-hour mark and I swear to this day that it cost us a try. David Burcher, the Newport centre who'd been chosen in place of Ian McGeechan, kicked for the corner and I have no doubt I would have got there and scored, had I been able to slip through the gears into overdrive.

Doing that with a pulled thigh muscle is a physical impossibility. I went off right away and shortly after half-time Brynmor joined me with a hamstring problem. We were replaced by 'Geech' and his fellow-Scot, Dougie Morgan but the game kept slipping away from us.

The very highest level of sport is all about making the most of opportunities. The Lions did that brilliantly in 1971 and again in 1974. They should have made it three victorious tours in a row because the All Blacks in 1977 were there for the taking. The blunt truth is that we were not good enough to take them.

Spirits sank very low after the third Test. By the time we flew to our next destination, Whangarei, for the penultimate match of the trip, against Bay of Plenty, a lot of the players couldn't wait to get home. We went into the team room to be greeted by a large polystyrene sign saying: Welcome to the Lions. Bobby Windsor's reaction summed up the general mood.

He took a run at the sign and smashed it into pieces which were then set on fire. Someone came in with an extinguisher and put it out before any damage was done. We won the match 23–16 and returned to Auckland for the fourth and final Test and the chance of squaring the series.

Unlike the hotel in Whangarei, we did not escape the most damaging of defeats. It all came down to the last moments of the last Test at Eden Park which I missed because of the thigh injury. Cobner's pack had made such a mess of the All Black scrum that they gave it up as a bad job and made the set-piece a farce by cutting their eight down to three.

With a front row and nothing behind it, they strung the other 12 players out in a thick black line and defied us to find a way through. Tactically, we didn't help ourselves. We'd become too forward-obsessed for our own good. It was all very well shoving the opposition 30 metres but what little ball the backs got was too slow so that 'Benny', 'Geech' and Steve Fenwick had no chance of doing anything constructive with it.

We lost that fourth Test because Phil missed a kick to touch in the dying seconds. You are talking here about one of the all-time greats, someone I played with at the highest level for the best part of ten years. Over that period I don't think I ever saw him miss a kick to touch.

Phil took a lot of flak but you cannot blame him. The team and the management didn't play their part in easing the burden placed on him. Fran Cotton and I often reminisce and we both regret that we, the Test players, didn't take more control and sort the problems out instead of allowing them to fester. At the time, it wasn't the done thing to complain.

In those last few seconds of the last Test, Phil's confidence at the end of a very difficult tour was at rock bottom. He had become a shadow of his real self and the Blacks made the most of that miss, launching one last attack which ended in Lawrie Knight going over in the corner for the decisive try.

To say we were the better side sounds too hollow for words when you've lost the series 3–1. Why did it happen? Many factors contributed to our downfall. The management – George 'Dod' Burrell, a former Scottish international referee, and John Dawes – was certainly questionable.

They were responsible for waging a war with the press – British as well as New Zealand – which they were never going to win. And that conflict affected morale throughout the camp. John ought to have taken a leaf out of Carwyn James' book of how to win friends and influence people.

It was all very confusing because John was a rugby expert of great experience who had won Triple Crowns and Grand Slams before the tour and who went on to win more Triple Crowns and another Grand Slam after it.

In New Zealand, I don't think John was equipped to handle the torrent of criticism from journalists covering the tour. Why didn't we have a public relations man with us? A good one would have headed off a lot of the confrontation and smoothed things over for the good of the entire Lions party. They wouldn't give us a doctor so there was no chance of a PR man being on board even if the request had been made.

Carwyn was a past master in the art of getting everyone to

sing from the same hymn sheet. He'd welcome the journalists, make them feel at home and explain what was going on. His whole aim was to get them on-side and keep them there. Dawes' attitude was to explain nothing and keep them at arm's length.

It got so bad that the coach saw fit to order Mervyn Davies, his great pal from the early days at London Welsh, to leave the team room. Merve had been invited there by Allan Martin but Merve was working for the *Daily Mirror* and he had been critical of the Lions, so an embarrassing scene ensued.

Crucially, we missed some very big players who would have made all the difference, not simply because of their ability on the field but because of their influence in team affairs off the field. Ian McLauchlan was one, Gareth Edwards another, and JPR a third.

McLauchlan wasn't picked, Gareth and JPR made themselves unavailable. This is no criticism of the players who replaced them. Brynmor Williams, then uncapped, played well after a slow start at scrum-half, while Andy Irvine at full back was the star of the tour.

Nobody got homesick on the previous tour in South Africa because the manager, Alun Thomas, and the coach, Syd Millar, organised the trip in such a way that the players were kept happy.

John Dawes had been massively successful as captain of Wales and the Lions, then as coach of Wales. During that soggy New Zealand winter of 1977, he was having to face failure for the first time. As for Burrell, being a committee man on the Scottish Rugby Union hardly qualified him for such an international role as Lions manager.

JPR has since admitted to me that he made a mistake in not making himself available. Gareth had been on so many tours that he found it impossible to ask his employers for more time off but he still cared to the extent that he wrote to me at various stages of the tour, asking how it was going. It turned out to be a good tour to miss.

It also marked the end of British rugby's brief rule over the Southern Hemisphere. Our game was changing and changing for the worse, into a forward-dominated one and it would take us until the end of the 1980s to produce a Lions squad capable of winning south of the Equator.

The '77 All Blacks were very average by New Zealand standards, not as good as they had been six years before. They were definitely mediocre compared to the team under Andy Dalton's captaincy that whitewashed the Lions six years later. There was nobody in '77 that we feared and yet we lost. Even now I find that hard to accept.

After nearly four months of mud and rain, we left New Zealand behind and the spontaneous roar as we took off from Auckland airport summed up the mood. I didn't join in the roar. I enjoyed the tour but I, too, had a regret – that we couldn't start all over again and avoid repeating the mistakes.

We flew to Fiji and revelled in the warmth of Suva. Even then, we still incurred the wrath of the management, this time over nothing more sinister than a few of us accepting a dinner invitation from a number of the Fleet Street reporters who had been covering the tour.

Fran, Gordon Brown, Tony Neary, 'Benny' and myself enjoyed a convivial night out which at least got us out of the team environment for a few hours. Back at the hotel, Burrell and Dawes gave us an almighty rollicking. They demanded to know why we'd had dinner with the gentlemen of Her Majesty's Press as if we were guilty of having committed a serious crime like treason.

And then we lost the match to Fiji. We were driven to the ground in an open-top bus with hundreds lining the route, cheering us on our way as if we were going to a carnival. So many wanted to see the Lions that they were hanging from the coconut trees and taking any other vantage point they could find.

The whole occasion was bizarre. 'Benny' played on the wing because we were short of fit players but maybe the most bizarre sight of all was 'Broonie' sitting on the bench with an iced lolly and a big floppy sun hat. He came on for the last ten minutes and made more history as the first Lion to play in brown ankle socks because we had run out of the official socks.

The threadbare state of the Lions' kit was another black mark against the management and the tour organisers, the Four Home Unions' Tours Committee. They gave us two jerseys each which were meant to last for the whole tour of 26 matches.

The baggage people must have borrowed a few sewing machines because they were stitching the jerseys back together again almost from the start. All it required would have been a phone call to the manufacturers requesting a new set of jerseys, shorts and socks but that would have been asking too much because it would have meant doing the players a favour. Through no fault of our own we were probably the scruffiest Lions.

That's how they treated us and that treatment continued after we'd got back home. We'd hardly got time to get over the jet lag than the request came for the Lions to reassemble at the start of the season to play the Barbarians at Twickenham in honour of the Queen's Jubilee.

We decided that we were being taken advantage of and that the time had come to make a stand. We declined the offer and told those running the Lions: 'We're not interested.'

They responded straight away. 'You must turn out,' they told us. 'It's your duty.'

Duty? What duty? As amateur players, we were beholden to nobody. We'd all busted a gut in New Zealand for the cause and felt we'd had no backing in return from the Four Home Unions. It made us feel that once we took off from Heathrow we really were alone – 30 players against an entire country.

Our management gave us the impression they weren't fighting our corner, although maybe they felt as vulnerable as we did. All that tended to harden our attitude because if we didn't ask for a favour, we certainly wouldn't get one.

We weren't exactly a bunch of rebels but if the Lions were adamant that we *had* to play, then we were entitled to expect something in return. We said we would play provided or wives, or girlfriends in the case of single players, could come with us to London for the weekend, all expenses paid. The second condition was that they gave us a new Lions jersey.

We were hardly asking for a King's ransom to play in the Queen's match. They said: 'No wives and you must wear the Lions jersey you wore on tour.'

We dug our heels in and refused to budge. In the end, the Lions saw reason and averted the embarrassment of having a boycott on their hands. Our wives were allowed to join us and we did get a new set of jerseys. The blazers should have made that clear from the outset as a small gesture towards the players instead of goading us into considering strike action.

And, after all that, I missed the match, played before a jam-packed Twickenham on 10 September 1977. The Lions put out almost the entire team from the last Test against the All Blacks and the Barbarians lined up with the usual galaxy of stars, not least the French back row forwards Jean-Pierre Rives and Jean-Pierre Bastiat.

Their team also contained no fewer than seven Welshmen – Gareth, JPR, Gerald, Ray Gravell, Geoff Wheel, Mike Knill and the uncapped Swansea outside half, David Richards. The Lions, with Steve Fenwick outstanding, turned on the style and won 23–14 – a belated glimpse of what might have been in New Zealand if only we had got it all together.

CHAPTER 10

Truly Unbelievable

Peter Jackson

JIMMY CANNON, ONE of America's most popular sportswriters who belonged to a largely pre-television era when newspapers sold in multi millions, described the renowned world heavyweight champion Joe Louis in revered tones as 'a credit to his race, the human race'.

They could have said the same of Ray Gravell and not a word would have sounded out of place. On a crisp Thursday afternoon in late autumn 2007, they descended on Stradey Park in their thousands to pay their last respects to a much-loved member of the human race.

His sudden death, at the age of 56, came on the 35th anniversary of Llanelli's victory over the All Blacks on 31 October 1972. Some of his old team-mates, who only a few weeks earlier had been revelling in his company at a reunion to celebrate the famous day, were now bearing him on his final journey.

They carried the coffin, draped in the Welsh flag, past the red brick scoreboard at the Pwll end of the ground. The clock had been turned back so that the result which had reverberated around the world stood there once more in silent homage:

Llanelli 9, Seland Newydd 3.

Almost 10,000, amongst them a who's who of British and Irish Lions, were there to bid him farewell in the crisp, wintry sunshine. Never, in his wildest dreams, could 'Grav' have imagined that he had touched so many lives and left such an indelible mark.

His was a send-off fit for the Warrior Prince, from the Llanelli Male Voice Choir, the Burry Port town band and, most movingly of all, from the folk singer Dafydd Iwan who dedicated a song about Owain Glyndŵr to the Gravell family:

'Myn Duw, Mi a Wn y Daw' (My God, I Know He Will Come).

The buccaneering centre from Mynydd-y-Garreg, the 'Rocky Mountain' village of his native Carmarthenshire, left a thousand anecdotes, like the one from the set of *Rebecca's Daughters*, based on a story by Dylan Thomas and filmed in Wales in 1992.

JJ

AN AWFUL LOT has been said and written about Ray Gravell – husband, father, rugby international, film star, broadcaster, Welsh nationalist, nervous wreck and world-class hypochondriac. In short, he was without doubt the most amazing character I have ever met in any walk of life.

He was also, again without any doubt, the most insecure. 'Grav' needed constant reassurance, to the point where he would drive you up the wall and round the bend. His insecurity has been well documented but there is one story about Ray Gravell, as amazing as the man himself, that has not been told – he owes his whole international career to me.

First I must set the scene. It is roughly four o'clock in the morning of Friday, 17 January 1975, in a room on the third floor of the Angel Hotel in Cardiff. The Wales team is supposed to be fast asleep before leaving for Paris and the opening match of the Five Nations Championship.

As is the tradition, we do not have a room of our own but

are sharing with a team-mate. I have struggled to get to sleep because when they made the rooming list, I drew the shortest straw. I am sharing with Ray Gravell and have at last managed to stop him jabbering and at least I'm asleep. That blissful state does not last long.

I am woken up by the sound of 'Grav' calling my name. I open my eyes and see him standing in front of me, wearing his overcoat and carrying his Gola bag with his kit stuffed inside. I look at him and say: 'Where are you going?'

He says: 'JJ, I've had enough. I can't take this pressure. I want to go back home to Mynydd-y-Garreg to Mam and Toodles.' Toodles was the name of his cat.

So I look at him again and say: 'Grav. For f***'s sake. Get back to bed and get some sleep.'

I could tell he was in an emotional state but I wasn't in any mood for a psychological debate. He kept insisting he had to go; I kept telling him not to be so effing stupid and eventually he got undressed, went back to bed, and the rest is history. I often wonder how different life would have been for him had I reacted differently when he said he was going home.

Suppose I'd said to him: 'If you feel you have to go, go, and don't forget to close the door behind you.'

He'd have been a goner. Roy Bergiers would have been called up to fill the centre vacancy and play alongside another new cap, Steve Fenwick. As coach, Clive Rowlands would not have put up with any nonsense. If a Welsh player walked out at four o'clock in the morning because he didn't want to play, Clive wouldn't have bothered with him again.

'Grav's' international career would have been over before it started. We talked about that incident a few years later when he was an established international and he tried to brush it off: 'JJ, don't worry I'd have been OK.'

The truth is that he wouldn't. He'd have gone home to Mam and Toodles and that would have been that. We all loved him because it was impossible not to, but to spend any length of time with him never failed to leave you in a state of exasperation.

Clive had made the decision to put 'Grav' and I together on the reasonable grounds that we played for the same club and therefore knew each other. I suffered this arrangement for a little until I could suffer no more. 'Grav' went in then with Geoff Wheel, although what the Swansea second row had done to deserve it I do not know. I then went to room with someone sensible.

When he wasn't getting up in the middle of the night, 'Grav' would be convincing himself that he was in the grip of some deadly illness. He called JPR 'The Doc' and made a point of knocking on his door to check out the latest imaginary tropical disease he was suffering from. JPR, in his abrasive manner, would answer the door and say: 'Go away, silly boy.'

Another doctor, Jack Matthews, the powerful Wales and Lions centre of the immediate post-war era, gave 'Grav' equally short shrift during the Lions tour of South Africa in 1980. Jack went as the team doctor and whenever Raymond woke him up to complain about some imaginary ailment, Jack would tell him to go forth and multiply.

We often suspected that there was nothing wrong with him at all, that it was all part of his insecurity. I remember one example of that early in 1980 when Llanelli played Newport at Rodney Parade which 'Grav' missed because of a so-called shoulder injury.

That meant he wouldn't be going head-to-head with one of his main rivals for the Lions tour at the end of that season, David Burcher of Newport. Phil Bennett and I had tried to convince 'Grav' that he had to play because if he didn't, he might not get the nod for the Lions. He refused to listen, holding on to his shoulder as if it was about to drop out of its socket.

Newport, the better side, won by a hefty margin. We got changed and retreated to the dining room at Rodney Parade for a bite to eat. The mobile phone was still some years from being dreamt up and the only phone within earshot was one which the kitchen staff used. We hadn't even started licking our wounds when one of the cooks came over to where I was eating.

'Are you JJ Williams?' he said and I nodded. 'It's for you.'

He stretched the cord of the phone about as far as it would go and handed it to me. It was 'Grav'.

'JJ, how did it go?'

'We lost, 26–10.'

'How did Dai Burcher play?'

'Quite well.'

'Did he get any tries?'

'Yes – three.'

At that point the phone went dead. A minute later it rang and again one of the cooks stretched it over to me. 'Grav' was back and this time he was ranting.

'How can you do this to me? How could you let him score three tries? You're all ganging up on me. You don't care about me. This is treason...'

And so it went on. It sounds funny except that at the time it wasn't. He genuinely believed there was a plot to do him down and that I was part of it. Ray probably wouldn't have slept that night either, worrying about whether the Lions would pick him. As it worked out, they didn't pick him, not because of any nonsensical plot but because he hadn't played much as a result of injury.

Ray was a hypochondriac of the highest order. Once, when Llanelli played Cardiff at the Arms Park, Gareth Edwards 'psyched' him out of the game. Cardiff were given a scrum and before the packs engaged, Gareth looked across at Ray and pointed to his shoulder, as if to warn him: 'I'm coming straight off the base of this scrum and I'm going to hit you on that shoulder.'

The forwards went down but before Gareth could feed the scrum, Ray had called for the physio: 'I've got a really bad shoulder. I've got to go off...'

It was impossible to square that up with his reputation as a warrior who was afraid of nothing. But that was 'Grav', a mass of contradictions who would be absolutely fearless one day and a gibbering wreck the next, depending on the circumstances.

Even after rugby had broadened his horizons, he was still the most unworldly, wonderfully naïve man I ever met. And as for his sense of direction, well to put it bluntly, he didn't have one. Any journey from his home to Cardiff would have driven Marco Polo mental. It didn't improve with time. Years later, I made the mistake of talking him through the drive from his home to somewhere in Cardiff and he must have called me from every roundabout!

After he'd hung up his boots and before he began making a name for himself as a broadcaster and actor, Ray was given a job by my boss Mike McGraine, who ran an industrial cleaning company. He started by selling in his local area around Kidwelly, then he was sent to the Carmarthen area.

I asked him how it had gone. 'I got to Carmarthen all right, JJ,' he says. 'But there was too much traffic. I couldn't drive with a big jam of cars and lorries, so I went home.'

The next day I took him to Swansea to see the main buyer at the Mettoy factory in Fforestfach where they made the famous Corgi die-cast toy cars. We walk into his office on a Thursday afternoon and the first thing 'Grav' does is to reach inside his breast pocket, pull out a packet of Woodbines, and offer one to the buyer, who looked and sounded like a member of the English middle-class. He politely turned down Ray's offer.

Ray then asks him if he's going to see the game on Saturday.

The buyer explains that he is not a rugby fan but, to keep the conversation going, he asks Ray whether he will be playing. This turns out to be a mistake. Ray explains that he is worried about his shoulder and doesn't know whether it has recovered sufficiently for him to play on Saturday.

For some mad reason, Ray asks the buyer, a shortish man, to stand up. As he did so, Ray hit him with his shoulder, knocking him across the office and up against a window. And then Ray, oblivious to the idea that he might have caused the Mettoy executive any physical harm, asked him: 'Do you think I'm all right for Saturday?'

I have been embarrassed many times in my life but never more so than on that Thursday afternoon at the Mettoy factory. We made our apologies and left, not that Ray thought for one minute that he'd done anything wrong. When he saw that I was in a foul mood, he said: 'What's up, JJ?'

'What's up? You've just met one of our biggest customers. You offered him a Woodbine, you've flattened him across his office and you haven't sold him any chemicals. What's up? That's what's f****** up.'

His sense of direction may have improved down the years if only because it couldn't have got any worse. To the best of my knowledge, no Welsh players have ever failed to turn up for a rugby international because they missed the flight.

Well, it almost happened back in the late 1970s. I took the irresponsible decision to let him drive me from our hotel in Cardiff to Rhoose airport for a flight to Paris. For some inexplicable reason, I must have nodded off. When I woke up, I discovered that Ray had missed the airport turning and we were now bypassing Bridgend, cruising westwards on the M4. He didn't have the faintest clue that he was heading in the wrong direction. Somehow we got to the airport in time.

Considering he was a man utterly without fear on the field, he had a surprisingly fragile confidence. That was why he constantly sought approval for just about everything he did in every match. Did I play well? How was that pass? What about that tackle? He asked the questions incessantly, not because he wanted you to tell him how wonderful he was, although he never objected to that, but because he needed reassuring that what he had done was fine by the rest of the team.

He wouldn't come into the dressing room at Stradey for training on Monday nights. He would burst in, shouting out: 'Ray Gravell, 25 caps for Wales, British and Irish Lion.'

And then he'd say: 'Who's the best centre in Wales?'

And we'd say, if only to keep him quiet: 'You are, Grav.'

Then one day a funny thing happened. Radio Cymru, the Welsh-speaking part of BBC Wales, had just gone on air with Brian Davies, the former Llanelli, Cardiff, Swansea, Newport and Wales centre, their rugby expert. Brian suggested that Gravell was getting a bit predictable and that the Welsh midfield might benefit from the more artistic skills of David Richards of Swansea.

'Grav' heard it on his car radio as he drove to Stradey for the game. By the time he arrived, steam was coming out of his ears. This time he almost took the dressing room door off its hinges, hurled his training bag across the floor and let rip.

'You'll never believe what that b***** Brian Davies said about me. Says Dai Richards should be in the team. Says I'm too predictable. Too bloody predictable? Wait 'till I see him.'

There was next to no chance of their meeting taking place on the pitch. Brian, by then in his late 30s, was playing for his local junior club, Pentyrch and, as luck would have it, they had reached the first round proper of the WRU Cup. The draw was being made that night and we got back to the dressing room as the balls were being shaken around in the velvet bag.

And you'll never believe what happened. Llanelli, the holders, were drawn at home against... Pentyrch. Had the moon been shining on Stradey that night, 'Grav' would have been draped over it. He could not contain his excitement at the prospect of making his point as forcibly as possible against his critic. When the day of the match came, Brian sensibly withdrew himself from the firing line on the basis, I presumed, that discretion is sometimes the better part of valour.

We beat them 53–7 and even Brian will admit he wouldn't have made much difference. We had almost come to look upon the Welsh Cup as our own private property. There had been five finals, we'd been in them all and won the last four and there we were, off on another run in 1977 to another final.

We never got anywhere near it and you can imagine, therefore, that it came as a mighty shock when Cardiff knocked us out in the third round at the Arms Park, bursting at the seams with 15,000 crammed inside. There was no argument about the result, not with Cardiff scoring four tries to our one and not even 'Grav' could do anything about it.

Gerald Davies captained Cardiff that season and it says everything about the stature of the Scarlets that some of the more senior members of the Cardiff club considered it their greatest victory since they'd beaten the All Blacks in 1953. We'd won 26 Cup ties on the trot and this was only our second defeat in the competition since it began more than five years earlier, in 1971.

'Grav' was irrepressible. He'd often greet me with one of his favourite lines: 'JJ Williams – better wings on a blackbird.'

And once at Stradey when he arrived at the last minute to take his seat in the press box at the back of the stand, he'd greet all and sundry. Then he'd spot Bleddyn Williams, there to report the match for *The People* newspaper, and he'd stretch a hand out saying:

'Bleddyn Williams, prince of centres. How many caps did you get, Bleddyn?'

'Twenty-two, Ray.'

And then 'Grav' says, so everyone can hear: 'One less than me...'

Talk about playing to the crowd... Ray, of course, never went out to hurt anyone, at least not deliberately. There wasn't a malicious bone in his body or a devious thought in his mind so it never occurred to Ray that he had done anything wrong. He had a heart of gold and he wore it on his sleeve and everyone loved him because of that. He enjoyed huge popularity on radio and television and, for all that, he never lost the sense of insecurity which made him what he was – a complete one-off.

Charlie Faulkner was an amazing character, immensely strong, fit, always happy and very coy about his age mainly because I suspect he was older than he cared to admit. He was so different, in the nicest way, to anyone else I came across in the rugby world.

Fran Cotton and Mike Burton were also big mates of mine so nobody could accuse me of not appreciating the guys at the sharp end of the game. I spent a lot of time with Charlie in our years together in the Wales team and often shared a room with him which reminds me of one hilarious episode.

It was in Melbourne during our accident-prone tour of Australia in 1978. We'd gone training, Charlie got to the room first and when I followed him ten minutes later he was not his usual sunny self. In fact, he was very annoyed.

So I said: 'Charlie, what's the problem.'

He said: 'You. You're the problem.'

'Me? What the hell have I done to annoy you?'

'It's all that athletic warm-up stuff you do.'

'What do you mean?'

'I've pulled my hamstring and it's all your fault.'

'How the hell is that my fault?'

'Because I must have caught it off your f****** towel...!'

Well, you learn something new every day. Until then, I never knew that pulled hamstrings were contagious like German measles.

As a BBC pundit during the lean years in the 1990s when Wales were often a laughing stock, I was paid to tell it as I saw it. I wouldn't have done it any other way even though I discovered that it was a sure fire way of making lots of enemies.

Wales as a national team were enduring such a terrible time that certain things had to be said. Neil Jenkins got a fair bit of flak from me which made me Public Enemy No. 1 with the Pontypridd supporters at Sardis Road. For some reason, which I never quite got to the bottom of, BBC Wales always seemed to be sending me to Sardis Road.

I'd been typically forthright in my view a few days earlier that Neil should have been dropped from the Wales team and Arwel Thomas given the chance to show what he could do as a very different type of outside half. I knew that would bring another torrent of abuse raging down on my head.

Gren, the wonderful cartoonist, caught the mood, as only he could, the previous night in the *South Wales Echo*. He had a drawing of a ring of a steel around Sardis Road and the caption read: 'All police leave cancelled – JJ Williams is here today.'

I got to the ground early, had a cup of coffee, and did my pre-match broadcast. Then I slipped quietly out of the back of the stand and slipped back in again as kick-off approached, hoping nobody would spot me.

Early on in the match, a helicopter flew over the ground and one wag shouted out and pointed to the sky: 'Look, there he is. It's that JJ Williams, commentating from the bloody chopper. Too bloody scared to come down here.'

On another occasion, again at Pontypridd, I walked into

the clubhouse in the company of another BBC Wales pundit, the former Wales captain Brian Price, and I got booed.

Fans have long memories so I ought to put the record straight about Neil Jenkins, a fine man who worked tirelessly to make himself a world-class player and maybe the best goal-kicker Wales has ever had. But I have to stick to my guns. There were times when he did not play for Wales as well as he played for 'Ponty'.

At a time when the game in Wales was stagnating from its insular attitude, Cardiff and Swansea had the courage to do something about it. In August 1998 they took the radical decision of defying the Welsh Rugby Union by leaving the Welsh Premiership to play a series of 'friendlies' against the English Premiership clubs.

At least they were making an effort to see the bigger picture and should have been applauded for doing so instead of being pilloried. The first match of the season saw Cardiff at home to Saracens, a match I was really looking forward to commentating on for BBC Wales.

When my instructions came through on the Thursday of that week, it was to cover Ebbw Vale versus Newport. I protested, to no avail. Ebbw Vale it was going to be and I also had been given instructions to do an interview piece at 7.30am on the Saturday morning about the coming season.

Again I protested, again to no avail. I said I would be out late at a dinner on the Friday night and wouldn't really be up for an early alarm call. Again, they were adamant: 'You have to do it.'

The phone rang at about 7.29am. 'JJ,' a voice said. 'We'll be coming to you in 30 seconds.'

For some reason, I decided I'd do the interview lying in bed without opening my eyes. It was not, I will admit, the most professional way to conduct an interview but I still felt peeved with the weekend arrangements.

'Well, JJ,' the interviewer said. 'An exciting new rugby season starts today. What do you think of this afternoon's matches?'

'Well,' I began. 'Cardiff starting their rebel season at home to Harlequins ought to be a cracker for all sorts of reasons but I'm being sent to a boring fixture – Ebbw Vale against Newport at Eugene Cross Park.'

That was my first mistake – never refer to a match as boring before a ball has been kicked and for other reasons which will soon become apparent. A few hours later I jump into the car and drive to Ebbw Vale. I always had friendly welcome there, from the chairman down to the car park attendant but there is a first time for everything. When I got to the entrance of the car park, the attendant was blocking my way. He was anything but friendly.

'Boring old match, is it?' he said. 'You can park your f****** car down at the bottom of the hill and walk up.'

I duly did so only to run into another verbal blow from a committee man: 'If you think Ebbw Vale's boring, maybe you'd be better off not coming back.'

The match against Newport turned out to be highly entertaining which left me thinking: How could I upset so many people in a two-minute radio interview? That wasn't the end of it. Shortly afterwards, in the same autumn of 1998, Ebbw Vale made their bow in the Heineken Cup against Toulouse, then by some distance the most powerful team in Europe.

I said on Radio Wales that I thought the Steelmen were playing well enough to give a really good account of themselves and I swear I did not say that as a feeble attempt to repair the earlier damage. And the result? Toulouse 108, Ebbw Vale 16, although to be fair to the Steelmen they had the last word, winning the return 19–11.

And the moral of the story? Wake up before you do an interview!

Sport has opened many doors for me in my life which would otherwise have remained closed. One such door opened during the Five Nations Championship in 1976 when I was invited to be a judge on *Come Dancing*, BBC television's highly popular forerunner of *Strictly Come Dancing*.

I turned up, as instructed, at the Top Rank Suite in Swansea where Wales were competing against the Midlands. I've never professed to be a king of fashion but that night I wore a smart navy velvet suit and was duly welcomed by the master of ceremonies, Mr Terry Wogan.

I was there to judge the rock-'n-roll section and never in the history of *Come Dancing* can they have had a judge whose two left feet has made tripping the light fantastic a precarious art. Mr Wogan put me an ease before the show got underway by chatting about our up-coming match against Ireland.

'You'll be playing against Tom Grace, won't you,' he said. 'A fine fellow, Tom.'

I agreed and pointed out that Tom would be really gunning for me because I'd kept him out of the Lions Tests against the Springboks two years earlier. Terry Wogan had put me at ease so I had no reason to be suspicious.

He said that at the first scrum, I should look across at Tom, give him a wink and shout out a few words of Gaelic which, naturally enough, I'd never heard before. Terry helped me with the phonetic pronunciation and it sounded something like:

Pog mo hoin.

I assumed it was a harmless greeting and thought Tom might be impressed that I'd gone to such trouble to learn a few words of Irish. Well, if looks could kill! He frowned and shouted back: 'I'll kill you for that, Williams.'

We got on with the game and Tom gave me a tough afternoon. At the end, I went up and asked him why he was so upset. And then he explained to me that the phrase I'd shouted at him was an insult. The translation was: Up your arse.

And the moral of that story? When you don't know what you're talking about, keep shtum...

Moss Keane could drink for Ireland and often did. There was a time when he must have been drinking for England, Scotland and Wales as well as Ireland because it happened on a Lions tour. I know because I was sharing a room with him, or not as it transpired.

The 1977 endurance test, as posed by the torrential New Zealand winter and our own failure to win the series, the tour will never be found on anyone's list of the happiest Lions tours. Sometimes a social function would break up the monotony if only because it got us out of our training kit and into our Number Ones – blazer, white shirt, tie and grey trousers.

I shared a room with Moss before the first Test in Wellington and we left the hotel at midday on Saturday. I did not see Moss again until he burst into our room at nine o'clock on the Monday morning, still in his Number Ones but very definitely looking the worse for wear. He changed into his training kit rapidly and, stinking of alcohol, caught the bus with the rest of the squad. They must have felt they were in a brewery.

We'd only been going through a few drills for five minutes or so when Moss bent down to pick up a loose ball and collapsed in a heap. While they carted him off to hospital as a precaution, the coach, John Dawes, was not amused. Moss hardly ever appeared in the team after that and the tour still had over two months to run.

In the days when every rugby and football club had a trainer with the magic sponge, Llanelli had the daddy of them all in Bert Peel. Whatever the ailment, Bert had the answer for it, including his own concoction of ointment which smelt as though it was a thousand times stronger than Vick.

Bert, whose grandson Dwayne played many times for

Wales, even had what could have passed for his own surgery at Stradey. And as a raconteur, I can safely say he was the only physio I knew who had more stories than William Shakespeare.

All Bert needed was a white coat or a couple of men in white coats to take away his most regular patient, the man who always imagined there was something wrong with him – Ray Gravell.

Now before this particular match word had got out that Phil Bennett had been to see the doctor because he was concerned about feeling tired during the warm-up. The doctor gave him some vitamin tablets which may have been absolutely useless for all I knew but once 'Grav' heard about it, he wanted the same pills.

'Leave it to me, Ray,' says Bert who then went into his 'surgery' and told Ray to wait in the dressing room. Bert reached into a cupboard and pulled out a packet of Smarties. He then took out all the brown ones and put them in a bottle with 'Grav's' name on it.

So before the next match and every one thereafter for the rest of that season, 'Grav' would go to Bert's surgery and swallow what he thought was one of Bert's magic pills. Then Ray would burst back into the dressing room saying: 'JJ – I'm roaring like a Lion!'

All the players were in on Bert's secret except for Ray. We all knew they were brown Smarties that you could buy in any sweet shop anywhere but even if we'd told Ray that, he wouldn't have believed us...

What Llanelli did in the 1970s will forever stand the test of time – four successive Welsh Cup final victories, the defeat of the All Blacks and a very good draw against the Australians. And our win-loss ratio over the course of those seasons was nothing to shout about.

Admittedly we had a tough fixture list against all the top English clubs of the day like Harlequins, Coventry, Bedford, Bristol and Northampton. Those were the big cross-border Saturday matches which meant midweek fixtures against some of the lesser Welsh clubs.

Llanelli on their travels were a shadow of the team that played at Stradey. Phil May, the Welsh international lock who succeeded Delme Thomas at the age of 20, always used to say that when he crossed the Loughor bridge for a midweek away match he had fourteen strangers on the bus.

One of my worst experiences as a Llanelli player happened during one of those away matches, at Newbridge. Every trip to the Gwent valleys was a challenge but this one turned out to be ugly and, worse still, it took a place a fortnight before the Wales-England match early in 1977.

Because fire had damaged the dressing rooms, we had to change at a school behind the goalposts. And then we walked straight into a Newbridge ambush. They tore into us and dominated most phases which made it difficult for us to play our usual open game.

Trying to get on the outside of my opposing wing, I found myself forced into touch. I went to retrieve the ball. As I collected it, an over-hyped member of the Newbridge back row tried to wrench it out of my hands. I obviously didn't let it go quickly enough because he walloped me straight in the jaw, knocking all my lower teeth straight into my tongue.

The referee blew, there was a bit of a fuss and on came our trainer, the famous Bert Peel, all 5' 2" of him. In typical Bert fashion he said: 'Stop your moaning. There's no harm done.'

With that he put two fingers into my mouth and started to pull up all my lower teeth which by then were horizontal in my mouth. I could feel the roots snapping. Pain? I was in bloody agony.

Bert slapped a cold wet sponge into my face and said to Phil Bennett: 'He's all right – typical bloody wing.'

Then Phil told me to go and stand at full back for a few minutes 'to get your breath back'. I thought that was choice coming from him! I stood at full back for two minutes and walked off the pitch unaided, back to the changing rooms in the school.

Unfortunately the caretaker had gone to the match so there I was sitting outside the school blood dripping from my jaw, my teeth facing down my throat. I stayed there like that for an hour until the game finished. Can you imagine that happening to an international wing today? There'd be an army of people in attendance.

After the match, our coach Norman Gale gave the referee and the Newbridge officials a blast, not because Norman cared about the forthcoming England game but because he thought he had lost one of his star performers for a few weeks.

Once they realised the damage, the Newbridge club arranged for me to see a local dentist who kindly opened up his surgery to sort me out. The next day I went to the dentistry school at the University of Wales hospital in Cardiff where they placed a solid silver cast over my lower teeth.

I could have hit it with a hammer and it wouldn't have broken. I wore it for the next ten days and during the England game. At the hospital they told me my jaw had been cracked, not that I told the selectors. Had I done so, they would have ruled me unfit and drafted someone else in.

Take it from me, if you were out of the 1970s Welsh team there was no guarantee you would ever get back in because there were so many outstanding players. I got through the game without any trouble, we beat England comfortably enough and nobody was ever any the wiser about my fractured jaw…

I have been to some strange places and experienced some strange things in my time but never anything quite like Harare airport in the summer of 1998. I had gone there for the BBC as part of their coverage of Wales' match against Zimbabwe and was waiting in the departure lounge to catch the one flight of the week to London. I was going back to attend to business before returning for the South Africa match, and what a shambles that turned out to be, Wales losing 96–13.

My seat was in the third row from the back of the aircraft and I had just fastened my seat belt when all passengers, except those in the three back rows, were told to leave the plane at once. Once the commotion had died down, I could see what all the fuss was about. Everyone had to get off except those seated at the back.

President Robert Mugabe and his staff had commandeered the jumbo. Once they had settled in, we took off, not for London but Timbuktu, a city in the West African country of Mali. We landed close to the jungle and Mugabe was treated like a king.

Before he disembarked the red carpet was rolled out over the tarmac to the steps of the plane. Maybe I ought to have asked him whether he was a rugby fan but nobody could get anywhere near him. It was like a scene out of a James Bond movie. Once the president and all his men had been whisked off into Timbuktu, we took off for London in an otherwise empty plane.

CHAPTER 11

Superstars

Peter Jackson

ACROSS THE LUNCH table of a bistro in what used to be Tiger Bay, with nothing stronger than a bottle of still water for refreshment, Barry John answered arguably the most baffling question of his rugby career: Why did he retire so soon?

'I opened the extension of a bank and after I'd been introduced, this little girl came forward and curtsied. Everyone thought it was wonderful. They were clapping like mad. That was when it came home to me that this was all getting out of hand.

'If I needed something to show me that it had all gone way over the top, that was it. That is in no way meant as a criticism of the little girl but it embarrassed me. It meant that some people had put me on such a pedestal that it was as if I was from another world.

'Nobody could touch me on the rugby field and I don't mean to sound as though I'm bragging. I had to finish because of my rugby, because of what people had made me through rugby. It was all getting too much. I'd had a gutsfull.'

In that interview he made no reference to the fact that he had been offered a full-time job on the sports staff of the *Daily Express*. The archaic amateur regulations in operation at the time left John a choice as stark as it was ludicrous – take the job and professionalise yourself, turn it down and carry on playing strictly for the love of the game.

Some of those whom he left behind in a somewhat gobsmacked state estimated his loss to the game as incalculable. 'The world never saw the best of Barry John,' Mervyn Davies once said. 'He was just about reaching his zenith then. He should have stayed in rugby a damned sight longer than he did.

'I had no idea he was going to retire and even if I had known, I don't know whether I was close enough to him to have been able to persuade him otherwise. I think his early retirement was a mistake. When I had to retire I was thinking: I'm just getting the hang of this game. I can take it on to a higher plane. Barry would have done the same.'

JJ

BARRY JOHN AND Phil Bennett had a great deal in common. They were the greatest of all Welsh outside-halves, they made tries out of nothing, kicked goals for fun and played starring roles in the two most distinguished Lions' tours of the post-war era.

They also had something else in common. Both retired far too soon. Barry's decision to hang up his boots in 1972 at the age of 27 was nothing short of ridiculous. Phil's decision to retire from international rugby in 1978 at the age of 29 was only slightly less ridiculous.

Barry got out in such a rush that I never had the privilege of playing with him for Wales. He was the first superstar of the game and he would still only have been in his late 20s had he stayed around to ensure the 1974 Lions did to South Africa what his Lions had done to the All Blacks in New Zealand three years earlier.

Much has been made of his reason for getting out, that the adulation got to him. We all had that. Barry had everything going for him, a good-looking guy with an easy-going attitude to life, and one of the best players of all time.

I don't think money was ever an issue with him. Whichever way you look at it, retiring at 27 when he still had so much more to give was a very strange decision. I suspect he was given some poor advice and he would be less than human if he didn't wonder from time to time how many more great things he would have done had he kept going a little longer.

Barry's international career spanned five seasons. He could have lasted until 1977, long enough to have given him the chance of going back to New Zealand with the Lions when he would have been 31. One of my regrets is that I never got the chance to play with him because by the time I joined Llanelli he had left Stradey for Cardiff. He had a vision of the game like nobody else.

Phil managed six years with Wales before he called it a day as a Test player after the Grand Slam in 1978. That was a mistake. He should never have retired so soon. I think it was a decision made in panic because captaining the Lions the previous year had taken so much out of him.

In that respect I could understand him missing the Wales tour of Australia a couple of months after the Grand Slam clincher against France when he played like a dream, scoring both Welsh tries and converting one. We all knew Gareth Edwards was going to retire then, a decision which made sense because he had been playing non-stop for Wales for 11 years, from the age of 19 to 30.

Nobody had a clue that Phil was going as well. What he should have done was take a year out at international level and come back refreshed for two more years. Don't forget he kept playing for the Scarlets until 1982, four years after his last match for his country.

Not surprisingly, Wales found life difficult without the best pair of half backs I have ever seen. In the course of winning our second Slam in three seasons, we played some wonderful rugby and maybe that led some to think that the end-of-season trip to Australia would be some sort of jolly, a sort of reward for being good boys in the Five Nations.

I never thought the two-Test series against the Wallabies would be anything other than tough, and tougher than usual because they had given us an early warning the last time we played them two years earlier that they were no longer the soft touch they had been. Whatever the reason, we were in no state of mind for the challenge.

The Welsh Rugby Union did nothing to give the tour any sense of importance. We had next to no preparation. The Union gave the impression that they expected us to win as if by divine right when they should have been hammering home the message that Australian rugby was on the up.

We found that out when it was far too late and the whole tour turned out to be a shambles. We were beaten up on the field and off it. In the first Test match our captain, Terry Cobner, threatened to take the team off the pitch at Ballymore in Brisbane in protest at the one-eyed refereeing of the local man in the middle, Bob Burnett, a native Queenslander.

As tour manager, Clive Rowlands was furious at what he saw as a clear breach of the tour agreement, that Wales would pick the referee from a list of Aussie refs put forward by the Australian Rugby Union. The night before the second Test in Sydney, Clive was so incensed that he threatened to abort the tour on the spot and take us home.

A few of the senior players advised him that such a move would do more harm than good, that we had to accept the referee foisted upon us and make the best of a bad situation. As far as we were concerned, there were two more caps to be won and that was uppermost in our minds.

While we were in the front line 10,000 miles away, the WRU back in Cardiff gave us no backing. We were up the creek without a paddle. Welsh players have been burdened with a reputation for being poor tourists, introverted and homesick. I always argued against that because so many of my compatriots were highly popular tourists but I would have to say that events in Australia during May–June 1978 did nothing to contradict the popular image of the Welsh being unhappy away from home.

There was no denying that this was a miserable tour. It had a bad feeling from start to finish, a sense that we were letting our high standards slip. What made it worse was that we seemed incapable of doing anything to stop the slide.

It all strengthened my private suspicion that the great Welsh team was breaking up, that the Second Golden Era was coming to a painful end. We had made the most of the glorious coincidence of having about ten world-class players growing up simultaneously in a relatively small area of south Wales.

Some on the gravy train thought it would keep rattling along indefinitely, that as one generation of hugely talented players grew old, they would be replaced by a new generation of similar ability. Some on the WRU were too busy enjoying themselves to notice that the assembly line was conking out.

They didn't appreciate until it was too late that a group of great players only come along at the same time once in a blue moon. It happened with England and their team that won the World Cup in 2003. They were not just well drilled with immense forwards like Martin Johnson and Lawrence Dallaglio but, unusually for them, they had real flair in players like Jason Robinson, Jonny Wilkinson and, to some extent, Will Greenwood.

They never had to cope with the kind of dreadful refereeing which undermined us at every turn in Australia. The off-side line seemed to apply only to Wales while it didn't exist for the Wallabies. In the end we lost the series 2–0 to a drop goal from Paul McLean that should never have been given for the valid reason that it never went between the posts.

We even lost the fighting. Graham Price had his jaw broken by a punch from the Wallaby prop Steve Finnane and we had so many injuries that day at the Sydney Cricket Ground that JPR had to start as an emergency wing forward. Alun Donovan was another casualty on debut at full back and we had no subs left by the time I injured a thigh muscle. All I could do was hobble about on the wing, a passenger.

At the after-match function, Rowlands pushed diplomacy aside and spoke openly about Australian thuggery. Our hosts listened, shrugged their shoulders and saw us off as just another bunch of whingeing Poms.

Seven players got their first caps in those two Tests – Gareth Davies, Brynmor Williams, Stuart Lane, Donovan, Terry Holmes, Clive Davis and John Richardson.

They were presented with their caps at an impromptu ceremony at Heathrow as soon as we'd got off the plane. Why they weren't presented with them in Australia straight after the match as per usual, I did not know, but then nobody should have been surprised that a tour of cock-ups should end up with another. And we couldn't blame the Aussies for that.

You didn't need to be a genius to sense that the balance of power was shifting. The Wallabies, with outstanding players like Mark Loane, Greg Cornelsen and Andrew Slack, went from strength to strength. They completed a Grand Slam tour of the UK and Ireland in 1984.

Wales, by contrast, were on borrowed time. Losing Gareth and Phil ripped the heart out of the team. That was bad enough but worse was to come with other outstanding players like Gerald Davies, Terry Cobner, JPR, Bobby Windsor and Charlie Faulkner, coming towards the end of their careers. And I was coming towards the end of mine.

Season 1978–9 would be my last on the wing for Wales. There was still time for one more Triple Crown, for one more infuriatingly narrow defeat by the All Blacks and a controversy which has raged off and on ever since. I blame myself for the fact that we lost as I shall explain.

Before all that, two more retirements put two more holes in the Wales team. The season began with Gerald Davies, at the age of 33, announcing that he had played his last Test match, and the public was still coming to terms with that when Terry Cobner decided he'd had enough only a few weeks before New Zealand were due at Cardiff Arms Park.

That left Wales needing a new captain. JPR stepped up to fill the void in his inimitable way and after three years of few changes under just two captains – Mervyn Davies and Phil Bennett – we now had three in eight months. JPR led from the front and we all followed but there was more to his captaincy than a typical up-and-at-'em attitude.

He was good at decision-making, very good at motivating the rest of the team and just as good when it came to criticising the general committee of the Welsh Rugby Union during his speeches at the after-match dinners. He was never afraid to give them both barrels when he felt the situation required some straight-talking, which it often did, and then at other times he would be more tongue-in-cheek.

He also had the advantage over the rest of us, with the notable exception of Derek Quinnell, in that he knew what it was like to win a Test match against the All Blacks. Both had been part of the '71 Lions in New Zealand and despite the Lions failure out there in '77, we all believed that the men in black were there for the taking.

How often down the decades have Welsh teams thought that and come unstuck? This time we really should have stuck it to them and we would have done had I not made a mistake which has caused me a few nightmares. The mere thought of it is always liable to trigger another.

There were extenuating circumstances but in the end it came down to me and I failed to deliver. I'd always prided myself on being able to produce something to get my team – Llanelli, Wales or the Lions – out of trouble. I'd always succeeded until Remembrance Day 1978 which is probably as good a reason as any why I can't forget it!

Seventeen days earlier, I played for West Wales against the All Blacks at St Helen's in Swansea. I got carried off on a stretcher not, as has been reported, because I got raked by their forwards but because of a tackle I'd made from behind on their right wing Stu Wilson. In doing so I caught his studs and they caused a nasty gash on my left thigh.

Gordon Rowley, the elderly Wales team doctor, said: 'We'll stitch you up here and now.' The dressing room was not exactly noted for its hygiene, the doctor gave me an injection and then went to work with the needle putting in 15 stitches. The injection didn't seem to have any effect because the pain was something else but it gave me a chance of being fit for the Test match, or so I thought.

The selectors had no doubt because they picked me in my usual position on the right wing. I only had the stitches removed 48 hours before kick-off and I knew in my heart of hearts that I was not 100 per cent fit. When you are desperate to play, you don't rush up to the Big Five and tell them you've got a problem.

I knew also that against the All Blacks, of all people, you have to be at your sharpest. I wasn't. They gave me injections before the game and I went out on what you could describe as a wing and a prayer, hoping against hope that the gods would be on my side. They weren't, although for some of the match it looked as though we would beat them at long last without having to score a single try.

Gareth Davies put us 9–0 ahead with three penalties and we were still in front when my nightmare moment arrived. Terry Holmes had a great match at scrum half and if ever anyone deserved to be on the winning side that day, he did.

He made a terrific break during the second half and threw a long pass towards me on the right wing. Had I been at the top of my game, I would have scooped the ball up and scored. Instead, I let it bounce and then bounce again. By the time I got it in my hands, the great All Black flanker, Graham Mourie, had got across with a smothering tackle.

The chance had gone and, as subsequent events showed, a Welsh victory went with it. A try then would have increased our lead to 16–10 with a conversion to come and time beginning to run out. I still blame myself and I shall forever regard that as one of the saddest moments of my life as a rugby player. I should have scored and, as one who demanded high standards of himself, there's no getting away from that.

Had I done so, history would have taken a different course. The All Blacks would have had to resort to more than the notorious line-out dive to have saved their necks. Instead, the antics of Frank Oliver and Andy Haden in conning the referee into awarding a penalty from that line-out allowed them to cheat their way to a 13–12 win.

At the time most of us in the Wales team did not realise how low the Blacks had stooped. The referee, Roger Quittenton, said he had penalised Geoff Wheel for barging at the front of the line-out but the New Zealanders were convinced that the ref had fallen for their trick.

The television cameras showed the incident for what it was, a laughable stunt except that the only people laughing were wearing black jerseys with silver ferns. It was, quite literally, daylight robbery but how typical of the Kiwis to come up with a way of getting out of jail. Andy Haden hasn't lost a wink of sleep over people accusing him of a devious, dirty trick, made all the more so because it had been planned before the match.

It shows you how ruthless they are about winning – winning at any cost. They say time is a great healer but time has done nothing to heal this one. It is still a running sore and probably will remain so.

There is a lot of scope within the laws of rugby union for cheating but let me make this very clear. I would rather lose than win by doing what the All Blacks did at the Arms Park in 1978. Heaven knows we have been in tight corners in our time but I do not know of any Welshman who would have planned to do something like that. I do not know of anyone in British rugby who has cheated as blatantly as Oliver and Haden cheated us.

Once again, they got clean away with it and the record books will forever show that New Zealand beat Wales 13–12. There won't ever be an asterisk next to the scoreline to denote that the winning penalty should never have been awarded. Because of the way they did it I could never bring myself to say: 'Well done.'

The 1970s Wales team was capable of beating anyone in Cardiff. Why, then, did we keep losing to the All Blacks? One reason which tends to be overlooked is to be found in the timing of matches, always in late autumn and always a one-off match which meant we never had any chance to get into peak condition. Autumn Tests then were nothing like they are now. We never got our preparation right.

In that respect the players were short-changed. They would have had a fairer crack of the whip had we played New Zealand later in the season, in March or April after the Five Nations. We invariably finished the championship fit and firing on every cylinder but a spring fixture never happened and probably never will.

Throughout the 1970s, New Zealand held no fears for us. We always believed we had the team to beat them but since then too many Welsh teams have made the mistake of giving New Zealand too much respect and that has contributed to the fact that, by mid-2015, we still hadn't beaten them since 1953.

If my time at the highest level of the game was beginning to run out, at least they kept picking me because I was still worth my place. And I was able to justify my selection throughout the 1979 Five Nations by ensuring that I went out on a high with the roar of the Arms Park ringing in my ears.

No country, not even England during the 1920s when they won so many Grand Slams, had won the Triple Crown four times on the bounce, although England got round to equalling it between 1995 and 1998. On St Patrick's Day 1979 we became the first to do it and what better way of clinching it than beating England at home by the length of Westgate Street?

We'd won at Murrayfield, edged home 24–21 against Ireland in Cardiff, and lost by a point to France in Paris. Only England stood between us and a special place in history and we would have to do it without two-thirds of the Pontypool front row.

Charlie Faulkner missed out because of a knee injury and Bobby Windsor was in hospital recovering from burns to his back which he had received the previous week from the lime markings to the pitch at Pontypool Park. Neither would play for Wales again. Suddenly Graham Price was left to soldier on as the youngest member of the trio.

Looking round the dressing room just before the match, I saw how much the team had changed. Only one was still there from my debut at the Parc des Princes six years before – JPR. His very presence was enough to reassure everyone else. We all knew he had never lost to England and he was hardly going to break the habit of a lifetime now.

JPR had also stated that this would be his last match for Wales. As it turned out, it wasn't. I hadn't said anything about the England game being my last because I didn't see any need to make my mind up until after the summer. As it turned out, it was.

We scored five tries and Mike Roberts, brought back at the

age of 33 to fill the gap left by the injured Geoff Wheel, got one of them. David Richards, Paul Ringer and Elgan Rees all got in on the act and so did I – my last try on my 30th consecutive match for Wales.

Talk about going out on a high. This was higher than anything I'd ever dreamt about as a boy growing up in Nantyffyllon – four Triple Crowns and four championship titles in five seasons. It was time to take stock and think hard about my future in rugby because now I had more than Jane to think about.

We had started a family and rugby was no longer the driving force in my life. The game still mattered but, as my circumstances changed, less so than it had. In the autumn of 1979, Wales were looking ahead to their first match of another season, at home to Romania, and I was otherwise engaged in an international event of a very different kind.

Superstars on BBC Television drew audiences of up to ten million and I made my debut in one of the heats for the 1980 UK final which was being filmed at Cwmbrân Stadium and shown a few months later. To qualify I had to get through the qualifier at Grangemouth where, as luck would have it, one of my rivals was the Scottish footballer, Joe Jordan.

Terry Yorath, then Joe's team-mate at Leeds United and, of course, captain of Wales, took me to one side before the 100-metre sprint. 'You'll have trouble with Joe,' he says. 'He's the quickest man in football. If you're not careful, big Joe will have you.'

What did Yorath, never the quickest on two legs, know about speed anyway? I won the race and was very careful to leave Joe as far behind as possible. From memory, it was something like 20 metres which was a big distance and it was nice to get a little back on behalf of Wales against the man whose controversial handball in a World Cup qualifier at Anfield cost our football team a place at the 1978 finals in Argentina.

The final at the Cwmbrân athletics stadium, a venue I knew well, put me up against an all-star line-up that included the only striker to score a hat-trick in the World Cup final, Geoff, later Sir Geoffrey, Hurst. The others were all superstars as well – champion boxer Alan Minter, the 400-metre runner John Sherwood, the modern pentathlete Danny Nightingale, Olympic gold medallist Daley Thompson, Britain's best basketballer, Steve Assinder, and, from the world of judo, the man we all had to beat, Brian Jacks.

Hurst had qualified by winning the veterans version of *Superstars*. He'd have beaten people like John Dawes who wouldn't have been waddling too quickly in those days. Most of us turned up for a bit of fun and most of us had done hardly anything in the way of preparation but Brian Jacks had done plenty.

He brought a bus-full of supporters and a banner which read: Brian Jacks Superstar Ltd. The competition revolved around eight different disciplines. Each finalist could drop out of two and nobody could enter his specialist event. While that ruled Thompson out of the sprint and the steeplechase, I was able to take part in both because I was there as a rugby player, not as a sprinter.

I won both but did little else and finished fifth, behind Jacks, Sherwood, Thompson and Assinder but ahead of Nightingale, Minter and Hurst. It was an unforgettable experience and a wonderful opportunity to get to know some big names from other sports, none bigger than Geoff Hurst, one of my boyhood football idols. He must have been about 40 then and I could never understand why he would want to expose himself to serious competition from much younger athletes.

If only the opportunity had presented itself ten years sooner, I think I could have won it. There was decent prize money to be won in the final – £5,000 for first place, £1,000 for last. I think I got £1,500, not that I saw a penny of it. The money went straight to the WRU as a charitable donation, as had the £1,500 I got for winning the heat.

During a break in the final I had a conversation with Dawes about the coming international rugby season. He said: 'We've got Romania coming up in three weeks' time and we're not going to consider you.'

I told him I'd been on the verge of retiring since the England match and now I knew for sure that it was the right thing to do. By then I had already taken the biggest decision of my life. I had taken the plunge into the choppy waters of the business world and launched my own company.

CHAPTER 12

Tragedy

As the sun began to set on the 1970s as well as on my time as an international sportsman, two major events changed my entire way of life. I became a father for the first time and within two years I was running my own business or, to be more accurate, I was struggling to learn how to run it.

Kathryn was born on 10 November 1977 and I struck out on my own in September 1979. Jane had given up her job in teaching to look after the baby and run our home in Porthcawl which made it all the more imperative for my new industrial painting company to succeed.

Inevitably, it diluted my interest in rugby. I was still playing for Llanelli but the old fire wasn't there any more, something I learnt when Ray Gravell was doing his tub-thumping stuff as captain just before an early season match. He turned to me and said: 'JJ, I want you to die for me this afternoon.'

I looked him in the eye and thought to myself: Sorry, Grav. I'll do my best as always but as for the other stuff, it's not in my blood any more.

When the big matches came round, I found it difficult to make the adjustment from playing to spectating. I'd been an integral part of the Wales team for six years and when the 1980 Five Nations got underway, there I was on the outside looking in.

The omens were bad from the start. Wales won the first match, against France, but the president of the French Rugby Federation, Albert Ferrasse, made a big song-and-dance about

208

the Welsh forwards, accusing them of being dirty. When I saw that in the papers on the Monday morning, I had to read it a second time to make sure I'd got it right.

There have been plenty of cases in sport down the years of the pot calling the kettle black but France complaining about dirty play? France, of all people? During my time at Llanelli we never went there and the same went for most of the other leading Welsh sides. They loved the social side but the rugby was too violent so they gave it up as a bad job.

The England match at Twickenham that year, when we beat them 2–0 on tries but lost to three Dusty Hare penalties, has been condemned as the nastiest ever played between the countries. I'd played for Llanelli against the Army at Aldershot the night before and then found I couldn't get into Twickenham because I didn't have a ticket.

Funny, that. You play for years, make sure your nearest and dearest are looked after and then, when you're out of it, you can't get a look in. I was with my brother Peter and he didn't have a ticket either so rather than take a chance we decided to shoot back down the M4 and watch the match at home.

We got back in time to see Paul Ringer get his marching orders from the Irish referee, David Burnett. Of all the Welsh players who have ever been sent off, no early bath has caused such controversy as Ringer's that day at 'Headquarters'. Paul was a fiery character, a fine player, incredibly quick despite the fact that he suffered terribly from asthma.

He made the long walk for something which, compared to some of the fouls that had been committed in the name of rugby football, was relatively harmless – a late tackle on the England fly half John Horton. I've seen an awful lot worse go unpunished. As the row raged on, one enterprising individual cashed in on the mood by selling 'Ringer Is Innocent' lapel badges. I had other more pressing matters on my mind, like trying to make ends meet off the field and look after the family.

I was still playing for Llanelli and playing well but increasingly aware that the tries I kept scoring weren't putting bread on the table. Every sports person knows when he, or she, has had enough. Your legs, your lungs, and your heart will tell you when the time has come although some, of course, ignore that and play on too long.

On 20 December 1980, the Scarlets played Waunarlwydd in the second round of the Welsh Cup. We won 57–4, I scored two tries and left Stradey without any fanfare because nobody knew it would be the last time. I didn't even know. I could have gone on but in the days that followed, I decided I simply couldn't afford to give rugby the time it demanded. In view of what would knock us for six as a family, it was just as well I did.

Anyone in business will tell you that even in a favourable economic climate the first few years are invariably the toughest. That turned out to be an understatement. I was still fighting to get the business off the ground when we were devastated by a family tragedy.

On 13 November 1980, Jane gave birth to our second child, Anna. Everything seemed to be going well until one day just after Christmas I had a phone call from Jane to say that the baby had been taken to hospital and because of concern over her condition she was being transferred to the Hammersmith Hospital in London.

It was the most terrible time of our lives. I jumped into the car and drove straight to London desperately hoping for the best while fearing the worst. I was heartbroken. Jane stayed at the hospital with little Anna and by the time I left it was too late to drive all the way back to south Wales. So after all the acclaim of recent years, there I was in London alone with nobody to turn to for help.

The thought suddenly hit me: Where am I going to stay? I was just another lonely figure in the street outside the hospital. I racked my brains and remembered that an old friend, Steve Davies, lived in London and he kindly put me up for the night at his home in Balham.

The next few weeks were a constant worry over the potential gravity of Anna's condition and the lesser worry over whether the business would get off the ground. That's hard enough to do when you have the necessary funds but an awful lot harder when you don't have the necessary funds.

I was constantly wrestling with a question that wouldn't go away: Can I pay the bills? I've never pretended to be the cleverest man in the world so there was no easy answer, no magical formula. Peter Thomas, the Cardiff Blues chairman whose father started the family's famous pie empire, once gave me a straightforward piece of advice on how to cope with the downs of business life:

'When I have a problem, I sit down and work my way through it.'

In other words, you have to roll up your sleeves and graft your way out of trouble. I've always been prepared to graft and keep grafting, although all that seemed insignificant when compared to Anna's fight for her life which ended in March 1981. She was four months old.

We held a private service at our home in Porthcawl for family and a few friends, among them Gareth and Maureen Edwards. On this most distressing of days our grief was interrupted by a phone call from a bank wanting to know when they were going to get some money. Unbelievable but, of course, they were not to know that the funeral was taking place that day.

We took Anna in her tiny coffin and laid her to rest in the graveyard at Porthcawl which is where the rest of the family will be laid to rest when the time comes. Those who have gone through the agony of losing a child will understand the devastation we felt and nobody felt it more than Jane. Life goes on but you never really get over the sense of loss.

The lack of help from the rugby community did nothing to soothe our grief. Llanelli RFC hardly did anything for me at all either during Anna's tragically short life or in the immediate aftermath of her death. It left me with the conclusion that they wanted everything from you but gave you nothing back.

When I was playing for Wales and the Lions, everyone always seemed to be ready to give me everything. Then, all of a sudden, when I really needed a helping hand, it wasn't forthcoming. It was as if the rugby community was saying: 'Sorry mate. You're on your own.'

It left me, for the first time in my life, at rock bottom and I would have been stuck there a lot longer had it not been for one man's kindness. Stan, now Sir Stanley, Thomas, phoned me up one day shortly after Anna had been admitted to the Hammersmith Hospital.

He phoned me up one day and said: 'I've heard about your problem with the baby and I'm very sorry. If you need anywhere to stay in London, feel free to use my apartment in Park Lane.'

I have never forgotten Stan's generosity in my hour of need and yes I accepted his invitation and I did stay at Park Lane. It took some getting used to – staying in one of London's most exclusive areas and working round the clock to try and make ends meet.

Losing Anna affected me in many ways, including my outlook on life. One effect was to harden my attitude and it needed to harden because I was really up against it. I knew nothing about business and I made mistakes but I learnt from them and one of the mistakes I learnt from was to narrow the focus of the company.

I started out as an industrial cleaning company and then

went into the more specialist field of industrial painting. You name it and we painted it – factories, shops, offices, railway bridges, motorway flyovers, railings and sometimes houses. We have worked for, among others, Railtrack, steel and construction companies, oil refineries, local government and highways departments.

I had the advantage of being well-known and my name enabled me to get through doors which would otherwise have stayed closed.

I'd turn up on site to meet prospective clients. Most knew me, some didn't, and a few weren't too sure. One managing director said to me: 'Didn't you used to be JJ Williams? What are you now? A painter?'

The truth is that I've never picked up a paintbrush in my life. I pride myself in being a very good salesman and I leave the technicalities of the job to my managers. We had got into the painting business because when I was trying to establish the original work in industrial cleaning, a number of those I dealt with asked the same question: Why don't you paint it?

People gave me work because of my name and at one stage I was employing more than 50 people. That's not much good when your wage bill is so high that you have constant problems with cash flow and your profit is slashed. Luckily, I thrived on hard work and still do.

Often, during the dark times, I'd say to myself: What made you become self-employed when you could have worked for somebody else without all this stress and hassle?

Every time I asked myself that, the answer was always the same. I had an inner drive to be my own boss, to be in charge of my own destiny. You have to be able to handle pressure and live outside the comfort zone otherwise you will fail. I'd driven myself to be a successful international sportsman, now I was driving myself to be a successful businessman.

I never doubted myself and I was lucky to learn a lot from

my last employer, Mike McGraine, a super salesman. I became pretty good at it too, because I enjoyed meeting people and most of them were interested in meeting me. That gave me a flying start although a few potential customers declined to give me any work. They didn't say 'Who does he think he is' in so many words but that was the impression they gave me.

I worked long hours every day, seven days a week. Even with all that graft, we ticked along as a company for the first five or six years, not making much money but not losing any. It's only been over the last 15 years or so that we've made large profits.

One of the biggest jobs we ever did, painting railway bridges in Cardiff, was worth well over £500,000. We've had some great times and made some good money which has enabled me to enjoy a good lifestyle. I own numerous properties in Wales and Portugal and while I've made myself comfortable, nobody has given me anything for nothing. I learnt during the hard times that there is no such thing as a free lunch.

I suppose I am a millionaire so I can't have made that many mistakes because the company is still going strong after 35 years. I'm not as rich as my old Lions mate, Mike Burton. I'm not in his league but then who is? It's no coincidence that several others on that '74 Lions tour have also been highly successful in business, like Fran Cotton, Andy Irvine, Dick Milliken, Fergus Slattery, Bobby Windsor, the English centre Geoff Evans, Tom Grace and Chris Ralston, the former English lock who went into publishing.

I'm still managing director of my company. I still work every day. When people ask why, I ask them a question: 'What else am I going to do?' When you've spent your whole life thriving on hard work, it's hard to give that up and change your entire way of thinking. I suppose I'm still hungry.

I do a lot of charity work for many organisations, including being on the board of the NSPCC, and I would like to think

I've done my share towards giving a lot back to the game via the Welsh Former Players' Charity which is attached to the Welsh Rugby Ex-Internationals Association, better known as WREX.

There was never anywhere for the ex-players to meet at Cardiff Arms Park. Peter Thomas, not to be confused with the chairman of the Cardiff Blues, came up with the idea of a bar where they could meet at the Millennium Stadium which was then under construction.

That got me thinking about the potential of such a project. Once I get something in my mind, I am determined to see it through. I went to see Glanmor Griffiths, then *the* man at the WRU as well as being chairman, at his office in St Mary Street in Cardiff.

He gave me a tour of the stadium before it had been finished in time for the 1999 World Cup. During that tour, I said: 'Glanmor I'd like you to give me a room here where ex-internationals can meet for a beer.'

Glanmor said it could never happen because it would cost a fortune. We walked a little more and, on the same level just past the dressing rooms, there were some large rooms filled with nothing but boxes of memorabilia. I came across one which had an outside entrance and toilets. We talked a bit more but Glanmor kept saying it would cost a fortune.

In my earlier chat with Peter Thomas, he had mentioned that Phil May, once a team-mate of mine at Llanelli who had succeeded Delme Thomas and gone on to play many times for Wales, worked for Diageo, the British multinational drinks company whose revenue for 2014 was put at just under £14 billion.

I knew what I needed and while it was a lot less than a billion, £250,000 was still a big number. Would they be interested? I phoned Phil, explained the idea and said that if Diageo came on board, they would get 20 tickets for every match and 20 invitations to the WREX room.

'I'll talk to the board,' Phil said. 'Leave it with me.'

The next day, Phil's boss called me. 'When are we starting?' he said.

There were still a lot of hoops to be jumped through. When I told Glanmor that we had the money, he was not happy. 'How can you get that sort of money when we, the Welsh Rugby Union, can't get it?' he said.

I said: 'Because we are who we are.'

All we had was the shell of a room. Diageo's sponsorship would make it possible for us to turn the shell into a reception lounge with all mod cons and large enough to accommodate some 250 people.

The next obstacle was over a licence. Diageo insisted that one had to be in place for five years between the company and the Union. I talked to an ex-international, Bill Morris, a solicitor based in Newport. Eventually, it was all signed and the WREX room opened in front of the *Grandstand* cameras before Wales played New Zealand in November 2001.

It hadn't been an easy ride and while there would be more problems down the line, at last the ex-internationals had a room to call their own. Mervyn Davies became our chairman and Cliff Morgan the president. I was the honorary secretary and we had people of the calibre of Gareth Edwards, JPR and John Dawes on the committee.

For me, it is an absolute delight to see the old timers talking about old times, players like Windsor Major, who played for Wales on the wing way back in 1949–50 and whose birthplace, Llangynwyd, is only a couple of miles from where I come from, Nantyffyllon. On other occasions, it's been wonderful to see so many members of the great Newport teams of years long gone, like Bryn Meredith, Dai Watkins, Brian Price, Algie Thomas, Stuart Watkins, Peter Rees and Ian Ford.

But don't get the impression that WREX exists solely for ex-players to have a chat over a drink. In not much more than ten years, we have raised close to £500,000 for the Welsh Rugby Former Internationals Benevolent Fund, set up to assist those suffering from serious injury, illness and misfortune. We have helped ex-internationals come to terms with operations related to their rugby days, people like Roy Bergiers, the Scarlets hooker Andrew Lamerton, the Cardiff Blues centre Owen Williams and even dear old Cliff Morgan himself. Typically, he did not want to accept any charity, arguing that there were people far worse off even though at the time he was dying from throat cancer.

We have been delighted to have helped Paul Knight, ex-Wales and Aberavon prop, with his fight against MS, buying him a motorised wheelchair and adapted car and seeing him enjoy the international occasions in our room thanks to the support of the public. They are always prepared to support us because they know how willingly all these players put their bodies on the line for Wales.

I've also spent a lot of time in athletics following the careers of my daughter Kathryn and sons James and Rhys. That all three succeeded in becoming international athletes in their own right has been a wonderful source of pride to Jane and I. We have travelled the world to see them race, always making sure we were there to give them the best possible support.

As the eldest, Kathryn blazed the trail, initially at Llanhari Comprehensive School and then at Loughborough University where she was captain of the athletics team, an institution famous the world over for its facilities and roll-call of famous athletes. She wasn't just a very talented hurdler, good enough to compete against Olympic gold medallist Sally Gunnell at the three AAA's championships and win a Great Britain junior vest. Kathryn was also an outstanding musician who played the piano and harp at the National Eisteddfodd. She also did A-level drama and was such an accomplished actress that we thought she would have made a career on the stage.

Instead, she became a successful businesswoman in her own right, holding down a senior finance position at the Sports Council for Wales. Her husband, Graham Thomas, captained the boys' team at the Welsh Schools' Athletic Championships on the same day that Kathryn captained the girls' team at the same event.

That particular story has long become part of the family folklore, how he fancied her 'like mad' and she fancied him, also 'like mad', but they didn't speak to each other until ten years later. By then Graham had proved himself in first-class rugby, on the wing for Llanelli where he achieved something far beyond his father-in-law's reach some 20-odd years earlier. He scored a hat-trick on his debut for the Scarlets, against Boroughmuir of Scotland. He also played for Cardiff and is a schoolteacher by profession. They have two children, Joshua, born in 2010, and Olivia, born two years later.

James is completely different to his sister and younger brother in that he is not a speed merchant but a middle-distance runner. As a champion athlete in his own right he broke the family mould, winning a string of Welsh titles, including three in the 1,500 metres – in 2001, 2002 and 2006. He was also an above-average cricketer and golfer and yet the sport he chose, middle-distance running, was the toughest of the lot. He captained the UWIC athletics team and, as operations director for Welsh Athletics, he also managed the Welsh athletics team at the Commonwealth Games in Glasgow in 2014.

His wife, Imogen, is an international long jumper and triple jumper, and works as a physiotherapist at St David's Hospital in Cardiff. Their first child, Harrison Robert James, was born on 11 July 2015. As with Kathryn and Graham, athletics runs in the blood with James and Imogen.

Rhys, our youngest son, spent the best part of ten years as one of the very best 400-metre hurdlers in Europe and the

Commonwealth. He has the medals to prove it – European gold at Helsinki in 2012, silver at Barcelona in 2010 and bronze in Gothenburg in 2006. Rhys also won silver in the same city in the 4 x 400-metre relay, and bronze in the individual event at Delhi in the Commonwealth Games of 2010.

He will end up as one of the very best Welsh athletes of all time. In addition to his major medals, he is the only British athlete to have won European titles in the 400-metre hurdles at four levels – under 18, under 20, under 23 and senior.

His appointment as captain of the Wales team for the 2014 Commonwealth Games in Glasgow was due recognition of his status. Everything was going to plan; Rhys had just run his fastest time of the season, 48.95 seconds in Geneva, and I'd had a phone call from his coach, Adrian Thomas, saying that Rhys was in the best possible shape, mentally and physically, at his training base.

His brother James had been very busy organising the pre-Games training camp in Portugal in his role as manager of the Wales team. Just before they left, news broke that Wales' 800-metre runner Gareth Warburton had failed a drugs test which stunned everyone. Little did we know that worse was to come.

As the newly-appointed captain, Rhys gave a motivational speech to the team with particular reference to those who had not competed at the Games before. James called to say that everyone found Rhys' speech really inspirational. What happened in the ensuing 24 hours took some believing.

Rhys had just returned from early morning training when James rushed into his room with news that would bring his world crashing down around him. James had taken a call from UKAD (United Kingdom Anti-Doping) telling him that Rhys had failed a drugs test during a Grand Prix event in Glasgow a few weeks earlier.

Rhys' shocked reaction was to dismiss the accusation, that

somebody somewhere had made a mistake, that he would be the last athlete in the world to take anything. For James, as manager, it was the start of an unbelievably distressing time.

Rhys and his coach had to return home at once. James had the embarrassing task of smuggling Rhys and his coach out of the back of the hotel and then had to break the news to the team. He was so upset that he considered coming home but stayed after we had stressed the importance of his role as manager.

I collected Rhys and Adrian, his coach, late that night at Bristol airport. Both were in a state of shock and terribly distressed. Adrian, a retired headmaster from Glan Afan Comprehensive school in Port Talbot, is a highly respected and experienced 400-metre coach.

Rhys' other coach, Dr Wynford Lesyshon, formerly deputy head at Neath Tertiary College who has a PhD in analytical and organic chemistry, was a good 400-metre hurdler in his own right. They are men of vast experience and, more importantly, great integrity.

I brought Rhys home and while the whole world tried to contact us, a statement had to be prepared for release to the media. The bland statement was sent via Welsh Athletics and then the long fight started to clear Rhys' name. When the news broke, no-one could believe it.

Phone calls, texts, emails and tweets came in from all over the place in support of Rhys. He was, understandably, in a mess, pacing up and down the lounge of our home totally confused and heartbroken. We decided that the best thing for him was to get away, so he went off to stay in a friend's flat in the south of France.

These were dark times, not just for Rhys but for the whole family. To have a drugs slur hanging over him and by extension us, made it seem like our worst nightmare. As support flooded in on a massive scale, one message stood out. It came from my old Lions' team-mate, Mike Gibson. He said that if we needed legal help, all we had to do was to contact his son, Colin, at the law firm Charles Russell in Cheltenham.

At the same time I was being advised by a friend of mine, John Lister, ex-treasurer of European Athletics who urged me to find a leading QC in London with no expense spared. Our next move was to see Colin Gibson in Cheltenham.

We presented the facts and they started talking about reducing the automatic two-year ban to 12 months. We were adamant that we would not accept that. We were fighting on the basis that there would be no ban at all.

Through Colin and John Lister, we got in touch with Adam Lewis QC. Dr Wynford Leyshon's expertise was invaluable as we set out to prove how Rhys' training drinks had become contaminated with the minuscule trace of a banned substance which UKAD had discovered in Rhys' system. It was so tiny that, in layman's terms, it was the equivalent of a teaspoon of sugar sprinkled into a 50-metre swimming pool.

We had to identify the source of the problem which meant sending all Rhys' drink sachets away for testing. UKAD insisted they were sent to a certain laboratory which cost us £6,000. It proved to be money well spent.

One of the drinks, blackcurrant flavoured, was found to be contaminated. Six months elapsed before the hearing took place. Rhys and his coaches were ready for anything UKAD could throw at them. I sat at the back and was enormously impressed at the way Rhys handled the interrogation.

He was proved innocent and the only thing they could blame him for was that he could have taken more care with his drinks and possibly taken them to his family doctor approval. What a joke! Which doctor would have the time for that?

Throughout this ordeal, UK Athletics and Sport Wales were very conspicuous by their absence. At no time did anyone contact Rhys to ask if he was all right or needed any help.

Sport Wales put a block on all his benefits and even prevented him from seeing his psychologist at a time when he needed him more than ever.

Had Rhys been a rugby player, the team around him would have stuck close to him. Athletics just wanted to hang him out to dry and for that I shall never forgive them.

He was lucky to have had great support from his family, coaches and many friends. Sadly, had Rhys come from a family with no financial clout, he would have been crucified. How wrong would that have been?

How is it that Rhys and Gareth Warburton were deemed guilty until proven innocent by UKAD? Did everyone not know that an innocent mistake had been made by two athletes taking their energy drinks? Why did it take six months of heartache and enormous cost to arrive at a decision that could have been reached six months sooner?

It seemed to us as a family that UKAD wanted to make an example of someone and yet they invariably fail to catch the real cheats. Are they really fit for purpose?

CHAPTER 13

Laughing Stock

JJ

EIGHT YEARS HAD come and gone since my last international when I suddenly found myself back in the Wales squad, this time at the invitation of the coaches then running the national team, Tony Gray and Derek Quinnell. Returning in the early autumn of 1987, I found that the game had changed and that Wales were being left behind.

Admittedly, they had finished the first World Cup a few months earlier that year in third place. Some people made the mistake of assuming that Wales were now the third-best team on the planet behind New Zealand, winners of the first World Cup in their own back paddock at Eden Park in Auckland, and France, whom they beat by a 20-point margin in the final.

Fitness mattered as much as it always did, if not even more as teams around the world adopted an evermore professional and scientific approach to their preparation. The Welsh Rugby Union had been very slow to recognise that and the consequent slide of Wales from champions of Europe to an international laughing stock left them with an awful lot to answer for.

When I bowed out at the end of the 1979 Five Nations Championship, I did so as part of a Wales team that had beaten England by a record score (27–3), reeled off a fourth Triple Crown in a row, and retained their title as the No. 1 country in Europe.

In the eight years since then, I could not believe how far fitness levels had dropped until I saw them for myself. Tony and Derek wanted me to stop the slide and get the squad fit for purpose. They had also asked Lynn Davies, the Olympic gold medallist, for his expertise in solving the same problem.

Under the captaincy of Richard Moriarty, Wales had done well to finish third, especially after the hammering the All Blacks had given them in the semi-final. What alarmed Tony more than anything was the fitness gap between the teams. He had tried to do something about it but every time he ran the squad round the field a few times, most of them were on their knees.

Why had it come to this? The demise of traditional industries like coal and steel was one reason. Comprehensive education and the knock-on effects of the teachers' national strike two years earlier in 1985 was another, each contributing to the proliferation of the couch potato.

The problem, like any other, had to be addressed. The WRU, in their wisdom, didn't spend any time doing that. In their arrogance and complacency, they were still thinking as they thought in the 1970s: The good times will keep rolling because we are one of the truly great rugby nations of the world.

What a load of balderdash, or as they would say in many clubhouses across the country, what a load of b******s. There was one reason why we were great in the 1970s and one reason only, that a number of outstanding players happened to reach their peak at the same time – a freakish occurrence for which we were, and still are, truly grateful.

Now it had got to such a state that the national coaches were having to get the international players fit. The clubs had to take responsibility for that. Was it a lack of dedication on the players' part or a lack of knowledge from within the clubs of what was required for Test match rugby?

In readiness for the 1988 Five Nations, I took a number of

running and weight-training sessions with the squad. Many suffered badly because they were not up to it but some stood out, Jonathan Davies most of all as the fittest. Others were also exceptionally fit – Bleddyn Bowen, Ieuan Evans, Adrian Hadley, Mark Ring, Richie Collins, Bob Norster, Robert Jones and Dai Young.

That season Wales, captained by Bleddyn Bowen, ended the Five Nations playing France at home for the Grand Slam and losing by a single point, 10–9. That may have covered over a few cracks but Tony Gray could see what was coming and so could I – a trip to New Zealand which had the potential to go belly-up on an embarrassing scale.

Tony did his best but it was impossible to make much difference in the limited time before they left Heathrow. I helped him with some more running sessions at Tenby knowing full well that what was needed was an intensive training programme over a period of 18 months. We didn't have 18 days.

The tour turned out to be as disastrous as everyone feared. Test matches are so-called because they are meant to be tests of skill and strength between relatively evenly-matched teams. The matches against the All Blacks on the last Saturday of May 1988 and the first of June turned out to be a test of the scoreboard operator's ability to keep count.

The players went like lambs to the slaughter. The result was a demoralising reminder that the gap between them and the very best was as wide as ever. In the semi-final of the World Cup the year before, Wales had lost to the Blacks by 43 points in Brisbane. This time the hidings were marginally worse – 49 points in Christchurch (52–3) and 45 points in Auckland one week later (54–9). So in three complete mismatches, Wales had lost to New Zealand by an aggregate score of 155–18 and leaked a total of 26 tries.

True to form, the WRU reacted by sacking Gray and

Quinnell straight after the tour which was a disgrace. Tony, in particular, was a coach of far above average intelligence. He and Derek were a good combination. The only problem was that they didn't have the tools to do the job.

One example almost beggars belief. In 1985 Wales went where they had never gone before, to the Pacific Islands of Samoa, Fiji and Tonga. For such a venture into the unknown, Tony and Derek thought it essential that the team had their own doctor with them from start to finish and asked the WRU to approve such an appointment.

Their request was refused. Their ludicrous decision said everything about the WRU's concern for the well-being of their own players. The coaches should never have had to ask for a doctor in the first place. His presence ought to have been taken for granted with the general health of the squad of paramount importance. As it turned out, a number of players suffered head injuries and were duly ruled out because of concussion which is now one of the biggest concerns in the sport. That's how short-sighted the Union was 30 years ago.

Instead of backing Gray and Quinnell to the hilt, they blamed them. The game was crying out in its shame for a system to be put in place to ensure the players were properly conditioned. John Dawes, then in his full-time role of national coaching organiser, asked Lynn Davies and I to make a fitness video for distribution among the Union's member clubs. His idea was shot down by the WRU coaching committee.

It would only have cost a few thousand pounds but they refused to provide the funds. Dawes became totally frustrated as a result and understandably so. Who would have wanted to be in his position working for people who couldn't get it into their thick heads that these were desperate times crying out for some investment.

I also worked on the fitness of the Welsh Schools' and Welsh Youth squads as managed by Brian Nicholas and the former

Neath scrum half Martyn Davies. Both had very high fitness standards and some of the sessions were really tough. It was a start but whole areas of the game were being neglected and the effect was to undermine the conveyor belt of young players.

My brother Peter coached the Welsh Schools' under-19s for a time so I had an inside track as to the Union's neglectful attitude towards that vital area of the sport. Wales were forever changing their head coach – John Ryan replaced Tony Gray, then Ron Waldron replaced Ryan. What didn't change was the annihilation of the national team in the Southern Hemisphere.

A few months before the 1991 World Cup, Waldron's Wales were blitzed 63–6 by Australia in Brisbane, 12 tries to nil and again Welsh followers were very glad that the try had not yet been upgraded to five points, otherwise it would have been 75–6.

At the same time, England were getting themselves organised under the direction of Geoff Cooke off the field and the leadership on it of a young captain, Will Carling. The building blocks they put in place then provided the platform which ultimately led to England winning the World Cup in 2003. While England were heading on an upward curve, Wales were on a downward spiral.

Again Waldron, like Gray before him, knew about the fitness problem but had no time to be able to do much about it. Ron's Neath team prided themselves on their powers of endurance but, unfortunately, the gap between the club game and the Test arena was like a chasm.

By now it was painfully evident that Wales weren't lacking only in fitness. The skill factor amongst the clubs was a long way below what was needed at international level and I saw all that for myself week in, week out after I started commentating for BBC Wales.

There was plenty of *hwyl* but, as with everything else in

life, there is no substitute for skill and ability. I told as I saw it and people would criticise me for banging on about what was wrong with the club game. As a rugby nation we were beginning to accept mediocrity. I could not be a part of that.

Wales now were losing heavily on a regular basis and not just to the All Blacks, the Wallabies and the Springboks. England beat us 24–0 in 1992 and the following year we put in another pointless performance at Murrayfield, losing 20–0 to Scotland.

We'd failed to get out of our pool at the 1991 World Cup and would fail again at the 1995 tournament in South Africa. At that time a lot of good players, like Jonathan Davies, John Devereux, Dai Young and Paul Moriarty, gave it up as a bad job and went to play rugby league, an exodus which left the cupboard almost stripped bare.

On the field, disaster followed disaster. I've always believed that a country as fanatical about rugby as Wales is should always be in the world's top six. The grim truth was that we had fallen so far that we had instead become the No. 1 laughing stock of world rugby. I saw England win easily on the occasion of the last international at Cardiff Arms Park in March 1997 but something more depressing happened that day. It was the first time in my experience that 'God Save The Queen' was sung as loudly as 'Hen Wlad Fy Nhadau'.

When Wales had something worthy of shouting about from the rooftops in those dark days, their ham-fisted management were always liable to prevent it happening. A perfect example of that happened on 6 June 1998, the day before I had my Mugabe experience on the flight to Timbuktu. Wales had beaten Zimbabwe 49–11 at the National Sports Ground in Harare which was something worth writing home about because they did without virtually an entire team of first-choice players.

Byron Hayward had one of those debuts that players dream about. The Ebbw Vale outside half started the match on the bench until David Weatherly's injury left Wales in need of a full back to replace the departed Swansea man. Byron came on and scored a hat-trick of tries, a wonderful achievement which made him the man of the moment.

In my BBC Wales capacity, the producer in charge asked me to request a quick interview with Hayward before we lost the satellite. The request was made and Trevor James, the team manager, knocked it back. 'Certainly not,' he said. 'Byron must have a debrief.'

A what? Debrief was a word I never heard used about any team I played with. Debrief, so I learnt, was now a buzzword in the Wales dressing room. The management should have recognised that Byron had played his heart out for his country and deserved to be picked out for a television interview. Instead, in their insensitive way, they denied him that opportunity. What kind of management was that?

A worse public relations fiasco happened after the tour had moved on to South Africa. I had to fly home to attend to my painting business but I got back in time for the second last match of the trip, against Gauteng Falcons at a place called Vanderbijlpark, a steel town on the High Veldt.

It was there that I met Tonie Roux, a Springbok threequarter who had played in Wales during the controversial tour of Britain in 1970. Tonie said to me: 'I'm really looking forward to welcoming the Welsh party to our little place. For us, this kind of opportunity only happens once in a blue moon and we're really keen to give the Wales team the best reception.'

The international was still four days away but, for some strange reason, the Wales management decided to leave the Test team back at the hotel. It wasn't as if the journey to Vanderbijlpark was particularly long and it would have been more interesting than watching it on television in the team room at their base.

The match against the Falcons produced a total of nine

tries, 76 points and one sending off. Dean Thomas of Swansea had arrived about 36 hours before as a back row replacement for Martyn Williams, who was injured, and Dean's stiff-arm on one of the Falcons put an early end to his tour. If that was bad enough, worse was to follow after the final whistle.

I bumped into Tonie again in the clubhouse and he sounded more excited about meeting and greeting the Wales team than he had before the match. He had never forgotten the reception he and the Springboks were given after they had played against a combined Aberavon-Neath XV in December 1969. Tonie saw this as a perfect opportunity for one steel town to reciprocate the hospitality his Springboks had enjoyed in the Welsh steel town of Port Talbot all those years before.

Things started to go wrong at Vanderbijlpark on the field, as they often did for Wales at the time. They lost 39–37 and had a man sent off which, I thought, were two very good reasons for ensuring that they spent some time mixing with the locals. Instead, they turned what ought to have been a simple exercise in good manners into a public relations nightmare.

They did their 'debrief', which reassured me no end, and then they all jumped on the bus. Within half an hour of the final whistle, they'd gone. Once I'd finished doing a few interviews for South African television, I went into the clubhouse only to be confronted by Tonie.

'Where are they?' he said.

'Gone,' I said. 'Gone back to their hotel.'

He looked at me in disgust. If only the Welsh party had seen the disappointment on the faces of their hosts, they would never have shot straight off. They showed no respect for the traditions of the game and having a beer or a lemonade with your opposite number is one of the oldest.

South Africa in Pretoria the following Saturday, 27 June 1998, showed that Wales were even more shocking on the field than they had been off it at Vanderbijlpark. The last time

I had been to the Loftus Versfeld stadium, almost a quarter of a century before, it was to help the Lions to one of their finest victories over the Springboks. Now I was back to witness the worst beating suffered by any Wales team anywhere.

South Africa 96, Wales 13.

Live coverage on BBC Wales television made it all the more embarrassing. Some senior players stayed at home, a few went home with injuries and others gave the impression that they didn't want to know. We'd hit rock bottom, the inevitable result of the long years of complacency and neglect.

The WRU brought it on themselves. I lay the blame at their door for their blind failure to see that the system had broken down and do something about it. As far as I'm concerned, one of the biggest mistakes they made was to disband the Welsh Schools' Rugby Union, the heartbeat of the game.

Terry Cobner was director of rugby at the WRU when they took the schools' game in-house. Schools' rugby had been controlled by specialist PE teachers who had spent three years studying sports science and one of those teachers, ironically, was Terry himself.

A whole host of mistakes had been made by then, going all the way back to the 1980s. Who else but Wales would send their team to the World Cup with a caretaker coach as they did with Alex Evans in South Africa in 1995 and change their coach just before the 1991 World Cup as they did by replacing Ron Waldron with Alan Davies at ludicrously short notice?

Once they'd stopped laughing at us over the annihilation in South Africa, the rest of the world sat back and wondered what on earth had happened to Wales. We were so bad that the laughter in some quarters must have turned to tears because you had to weep for the predicament Wales found themselves in.

Why did they send a team largely made up of third or fourth choice players to face the might of the World Cup holders? At least one man rose heroically above it all, as you would expect of someone who won the Victoria Cross during the Second World War.

Sir Tasker Watkins QC VC did a magnificent job in his role as president, working overtime to keep morale as high as possible by rallying the troops. The chairman, Glanmor Griffiths, was understood to have left at half-time. He had seen more than enough and was off to catch the first available plane to Auckland to look for a new coach, Graham Henry.

It was a bold, decisive move by the Union, going out to sign up whom they considered to be the best coach in the world at the time. Henry, Hansen etc.

There is no denying that Hansen laid the foundations for the rebirth of Wales as a real force after all the years in the wilderness. A first Grand Slam for 27 years, under Mike Ruddock's coaching in 2005, was followed by two more in 2008 and 2012 under another Kiwi coach, Warren Gatland.

To his eternal credit, he took Wales closer to a World Cup final in 2011 than ever, a single point defeat despite the devastating blow of Sam Warburton's red card.

What I will never understand was why the WRU gave the impression of doing nothing to get just a few of their great players, like Phil Bennett for example, into coaching. Why was he never approached to coach Llanelli? Nobody ever asked him. Had they done so, the committee would probably have had him on turnstile duty as they did with such fine former players as Hefin Jenkins and Selwyn Williams. They had rather more to offer, I would have thought, than checking tickets at the gate.

After the heady days of the 1970s to rock bottom in the 1990s, Wales have come through the hard times to re-establish themselves as a force in the world game – three Grand Slams in seven years and within a whisker of reaching the 2011 World Cup final. How times have changed.

As you will have read, I have criticised the WRU heavily for the way they dealt with the players during the amateur era. Now, in marked contrast, they make sure the current Wales players want for nothing, in putting at their disposal the best training facilities, kit, accommodation, travel, and a even a cryotherapy chamber.

Nothing is left to chance and the teams have responded magnificently over the last decade. Unfortunately, all this has been largely under the guidance of New Zealand coaches. Like them or not, they have brought a ruthless approach to winning and the biggest difference between the current team and the one of ten or so years ago is fitness.

I was always criticised for complaining continually about fitness during my time as a pundit with the BBC. Now that we have caught up in terms of fitness, we have to make a comparable improvement in our skills. There is no doubt that youngsters in New Zealand, South Africa and Australia are better schooled when it comes to conditioning. My advice to the WRU would be to invest in schools' rugby, to give PE teachers across the country the facilities and finance required to raise standards. The teachers are highly qualified and I would recommend the reintroduction of the Welsh Schools' under-18 team with the teachers doing the selecting and the coaching.

The WRU has worked particularly hard under the outgoing chief executive, Roger Lewis, to put their house in order and the national team in the global shop window. The next step is to develop the rest of the game in Wales and build on solid foundations.

Do that and Welsh rugby will flourish for ever and treat us to many more magical moments. The Welsh nation, with its fanatical support, deserves nothing less.

CHAPTER 14

World beaters

NOW FOR THE hard bit – picking the best Lions XV of the amateur era and the best Lions XV of the first 20 years after the game went professional. I have therefore considered all the Lions over the last five decades. These then are my chosen few.

Best Lions of the amateur era (1971–1995)

15 JPR Williams (Wales). Fearless in every respect, his winning attitude never wavered no matter how tough the going got. Andy Irvine of Scotland would be my second choice.

14 Gerald Davies (Wales). The complete wing-threequarter. Pace and skill backed up by a sharp rugby brain. Of all the wings in the world since the 1970s, only Shane Williams came close.

13 Mike Gibson (Ireland). Most versatile back the British Isles has ever seen. Fly half, centre or wing, he filled every position with distinction. And his international career spanned 15 years, from 1964 to 1979.

12 John Dawes (Wales). Wonderful passer, a pleasure to have played outside him as I know only too well. Other centre pairs spring to mind – Sir Ian McGeechan and Dick Milliken, Steve Fenwick and Ray Gravell but Gibson-Dawes top the lot.

11 David Duckham (England). Outstanding footballer and lethal finisher who did everything in real style. When the occasion demanded, he could be just as good as a centre.

10 Phil Bennett (Wales). Barry John was a far more confident player and brilliant in beating the All Blacks in 1971. 'Benny', though, was the maestro – the most skilful player I have ever seen. He could do everything.

9 Sir Gareth Edwards (Wales). Out on his own as his record shows – 53 consecutive internationals over 11 years. The best of the other scrum-halves suffer by comparison.

1 Ian McLauchlan (Scotland). Always brought a massively professional attitude to his game. A real winner, ever ready to take a hit for the team.

2 Bobby Windsor (Wales). Not just a tough guy with a killer attitude. He was also a very talented ball player which made you glad he was on your side.

3 Fran Cotton (England). Immensely powerful prop whose footballing brain meant he could do an awful lot more than scrummage. The complete front row forward.

4 Willie John McBride (Ireland). Five Lions tours, more Tests than any one else (17) and more matches (70). Those records will stand for ever. No surprise that he's my captain, with apologies to John Dawes.

5 Gordon Brown (Scotland). So good that the Springboks tried to punch him out of the Test series and every time they knocked him down, he kept getting up. Superb athlete with the skills for any and every situation.

6 Derek Quinnell (Wales). Played in this position for the Lions in 1971 before he'd been capped by Wales and played there in a winning Test against the All Blacks in 1977. An all-round top bloke.

7 Fergus Slattery (Ireland). Dynamic player who makes the

team by a short-head from two Welsh contemporaries – Terry Cobner and John Taylor.

8   Mervyn Davies (Wales). Although the line-out was his specialty, there wasn't anything he couldn't do. Possibly the bravest player I have ever seen. The heart of a Lion.

Best Lions XV of the professional era

15   Leigh Halfpenny (Wales). Performances throughout the Test series in Australia in 2013 were right out of the very top drawer. Outstanding.

14   George North (Wales). Gets the nod ahead of Jason Robinson, not just because of his size but his power over 30 metres. Will become one of the greatest wings of all time.

13   Jeremy Guscott (England). High-speed skills, tremendous acceleration and awareness. Never afraid to back himself; England haven't had a centre like him since he retired.

12   Brian O'Driscoll (Ireland). Lasted nearly as long at the top as Mike Gibson and won more than twice as many caps. All the skills in the book and the courage to make the most of them all.

11   Shane Williams (Wales). Had the wonderful ability, rare among wings, of being able to change the course of a game all on his own. World Player of the Year says it all.

10   Jonny Wilkinson (England). Survived the kind of serious injuries which would have finished a lesser person. Kept coming back and deservedly won every honour in the game from the World Cup to the European Cup.

9   Mike Phillips (Wales). Strength and power are his great attributes, not unusual among modern scrum-halves, but Mike's competitive edge is second to none.

1   Gethin Jenkins (Wales). Massive work rate, not only in

the set-piece but in the loose where his pace and handling ability have proved invaluable.

2 Keith Wood (Ireland). Fastest hooker I've ever seen. An inspiring captain of his country, he was also a major figure in the Lions' series win over South Africa in 1997.

3 Adam Jones (Wales). The abrupt end to his international career cannot obscure the fact that he was the best tighthead in Britain and Ireland for a number of years.

4 Martin Johnson (England). One of the greatest players the world has ever seen in any era. Deserved everything he achieved, from the World Cup to all kinds of trophies with Leicester. My choice as captain of this team.

5 Paul O'Connell (Ireland). Johnson had a terrific engine but I don't think I've seen a second row with a better engine than the Munster man. Backs up his mighty physical presence with a winning mentality.

6 Lawrence Dallaglio (England). Like Johnson, one of the great forwards of all time. Power, skill and an iron will to win.

7 Richard Hill (England). A wonderful back row forward whose ability to play in all three positions has probably never been fully appreciated. Absolutely brilliant.

8 Scott Quinnell (Wales). Hugely talented, multi-purpose forward who knows the game inside out. A chip off the old block. Some chip, some block!

JJ Williams
Match Statistics

For Wales in official internationals

Date	Opponent	Venue	Result	Score
24.3.1973	France	Parc des Princes	Lost	3–12
10.11.1973	Australia	Cardiff Arms Park	Won	24–0
19.1.1974	Scotland	Cardiff Arms Park	Won	6–0
2.2.1974	Ireland	Lansdowne Road	Drawn	9–9 (1 try)
16.2.1974	France	Cardiff Arms Park	Drawn	16–16 (1 try)
16.3.1974	England	Twickenham	Lost	12–16
18.1.1975	France	Parc des Princes	Won	25–10
15.2.1975	England	Cardiff Arms Park	Won	20–4 (1 try)
1.3.1975	Scotland	Murrayfield	Lost	10–12
15.3.1975	Ireland	Cardiff Arms Park	Won	32–4 (1 try)
20.12.1975	Australia	Cardiff Arms Park	Won	28–3 (3 tries)
17.1.1976	England	Twickenham	Won	21–9
7.2.1976	Scotland	Cardiff Arms Park	Won	28–6 (1 try)
21.2.1976	Ireland	Lansdowne Road	Won	34–9
6.3.1976	France	Cardiff Arms Park	Won	19–13 (1 try)
15.1.1977	Ireland	Cardiff Arms Park	Won	25–9
5.2.1977	France	Parc des Princes	Lost	9–16
5.3.1977	England	Cardiff Arms Park	Won	14–9
19.3.1977	Scotland	Murrayfield	Won	18–9 (1 try)
4.2.1978	England	Twickenham	Won	9–6
18.2.1978	Scotland	Cardiff Arms Park	Won	22–14
4.3.1978	Ireland	Lansdowne Road	Won	20–16 (1 try)
18.3.1978	France	Cardiff Arms Park	Won	16–7
11.6.1978	Australia	Brisbane	Lost	8–18
17.6.1978	Australia	Sydney	Lost	17–19
11.11.1978	New Zealand	Cardiff Arms Park	Lost	12–13
20.1.1979	Scotland	Murrayfield	Won	19–13
3.2.1979	Ireland	Cardiff Arms Park	Won	24–21
17.2.1979	France	Parc des Princes	Lost	13–14
17.3.1979	England	Cardiff Arms Park	Won	27–3 (1 try)

Uncapped international matches

9.6.1973	Canada	Toronto	Won	58–20 (1 try)
6.10.1973	Japan	Cardiff Arms Park	Won	62–14 (1 try)
27.11.1974	New Zealand	Cardiff Arms Park	Lost	3–12
21.9.1975	Japan	Osaka	Won	56–12 (2 tries)
24.9.1975	Japan	Tokyo	Won	82–6 (2 tries)
16.10.1976	Argentina	Cardiff Arms Park	Won	20–19

Other matches for Wales

26.5.1973	British Columbia	Vancouver	Won	31–6 (1 try)
30.5.1973	Alberta	Edmonton	Won	76–6 (2 tries)
2.6.1973	Quebec	Montreal	Won	44–9 (2 tries)
5.6.1973	Ontario	Ottawa	Won	79–0 (1 try)
10.9.1975	Hong Kong	Hong Kong	Won	57–3 (2 tries)
18.9.1975	Japan B	Tokyo	Won	34–7
21.5.1978	Western Australia	Perth	Won	32–3
30.5.1978	NSW Country	Cobar	Won	33–0 (2 tries)
3.6.1978	New South Wales	Sydney	Won	18–0
6.6.1978	Queensland	Brisbane	Won	31–24

British and Irish Lions Test matches

8.6.1974	South Africa	Cape Town	Won	12–3
22.6.1974	South Africa	Pretoria	Won	28–9 (2 tries)
13.7.1974	South Africa	Port Elizabeth	Won	26–9 (2 tries)
27.7.1974	South Africa	Johannesburg	Drawn	13–13
18.6.1977	New Zealand	Wellington	Lost	12–16
9.7.1977	New Zealand	Christchurch	Won	13–9 (1 try)
30.7.1977	New Zealand	Dunedin	Lost	7–19

Non-Test British and Irish Lions matches

South Africa 1974

South-West Africa	Windhoek	Won	23–16
Boland	Wellington	Won	33–6
South-Western Districts	Mossel Bay	Won	97–0 (6 tries)
SA Federation XV	Cape Town	Won	37–6 (1 try)
Transvaal	Johannesburg	Won	23–15
Orange Free State	Bloemfontein	Won	11–9 (1 try)
Northern Transvaal	Pretoria	Won	16–12
Natal	Durban	Won	34–6

New Zealand 1977

Wairarapa Bush	Masterton	Won	41–13 (3 tries)
Hawke's Bay	Napier	Won	13–11
Taranaki	New Plymouth	Won	21–13 (1 try)
King Country/Wanganui	Taumarunui	Won	60–9 (2 tries)
Otago	Dunedin	Won	12–7
South & Mid Canterbury-North Otago	Timaru	Won	45–6 (1 try)
Canterbury	Christchurch	Won	14–13 (1 try)
Wellington	Wellington	Won	13–6
NZ Maoris	Auckland	Won	22–19
Auckland	Auckland	Won	34–15 (1 try)

JJ Williams for Llanelli

Matches: 227   Tries: 163
Debut: 11.10.1972 v Crawshay's XV
Last match: 20.12.1980 v Waunarwlydd

Totals in first-class rugby:	Matches	Tries
Wales Tests	31	12
Lions' Tests	7	5
Wales non-Test	16	16
Lions non-Test	19	17
Barbarians	10	17
Llanelli	227	163
Bridgend	100	99
Wales B	3	2
Wales trials	4	1
Natal	2	1
Irish Wolfhounds	1	0
*Glamorgan	11	13
Others	7	6
Totals:	438	352

*Estimated figures. No known records.

Llanelli figures by kind permission of Scarlets' historian Les Williams.

Bibliography

Bennett, Phil, *Everywhere for Wales* (1981).

Billot, John, *History of Welsh International Rugby* (1999).

Cotton, Fran, *An Autobiography* (1981).

Davies, Mervyn / Roach, David, *In Strength and Shadow* (2004).

Davies, Rhodri, *Undefeated The Story of the 1974 Lions* (2014).

Evans, Howard, *Welsh International Matches 1881–2000* (1999).

Fox, Dave / Bogle, Ken / Hokins, Mark, *The All Blacks in Britain and Ireland* (2006).

Griffiths, John, *International Rugby Records* (1987).

Jackson, Peter, *Lions of Wales* (1998).

Jackson, Peter, *Triumph and Tragedy* (2011).

McBride, Willie John / Bills, Peter, *Willie John, the story of my life* (2004).

McLean, TP, *The All Blacks* (1991).

McWhirter, Ross / Titley, UA, *Centenary History of the Rugby Football Union* (1970).

Reason, John, *The Mighty Lions* (1971).

Richards, Alun, *Carwyn* (1984).

Thomas, Clem and Greg, *125 Years of the British & Irish Lions* (2013).

Thomas, JBG, *Trial of Strength, the 1977 British Lions in New Zealand* (1977).

Van Esbeck, Edmund, *Irish Rugby, A History* (1999).

Williams, JPR, *JPR* (1979).

Windsor, Bobby / Jackson, Peter, *The Iron Duke* (2010).

Index

'A book celebrating great
Welsh victories over the English'

Wales
defeated
England...

LYNN DAVIES

£7.99

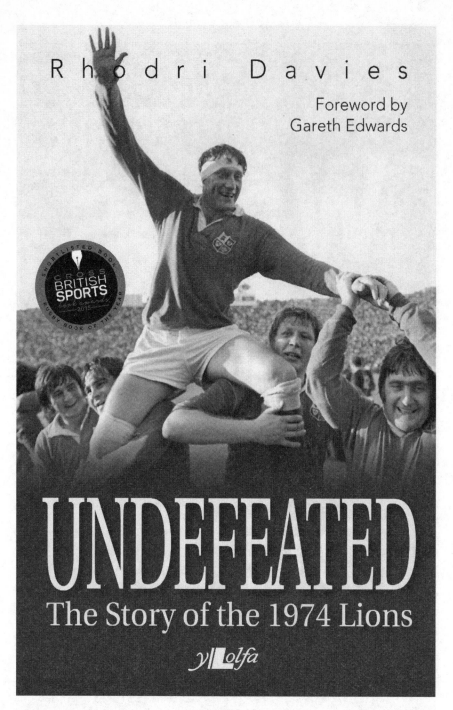

R h o d r i   D a v i e s

Foreword by
Gareth Edwards

CROSS
BRITISH
SPORTS
2015

UNDEFEATED
The Story of the 1974 Lions

y Lolfa

£9.95

DELME

THE AUTOBIOGRAPHY

yLolfa

with Alun Gibbard

£9.95

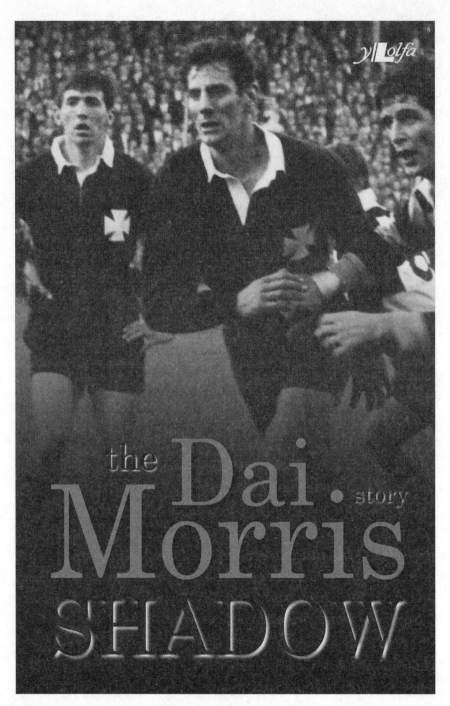

the Dai · story
Morris
SHADOW

£9.95

y Lolfa

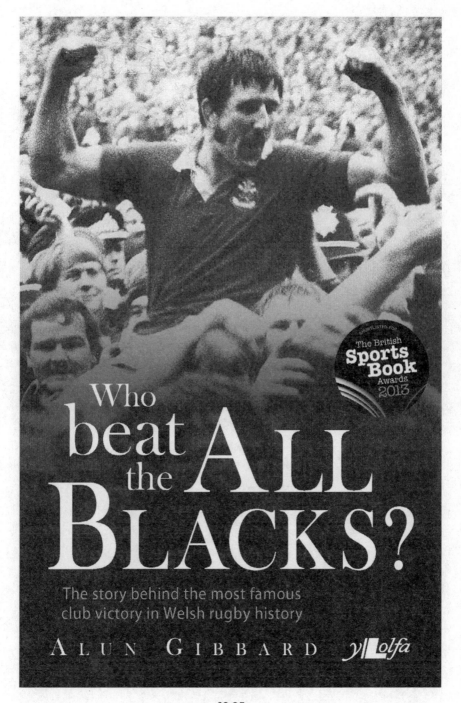

Who beat the ALL BLACKS?

The story behind the most famous
club victory in Welsh rugby history

A L U N   G I B B A R D   *y Lolfa*

£9.95

JJ Williams: The Life and Times of a Rugby Legend
is just one of a whole range of publications from
Y Lolfa. For a full list of books currently in print,
send now for your free copy of our new full-
colour catalogue. Or simply surf into our website

www.ylolfa.com

for secure on-line ordering.

TALYBONT CEREDIGION CYMRU SY24 5HE
e-mail ylolfa@ylolfa.com
website www.ylolfa.com
phone (01970) 832 304
fax 832 782